Spiritual Questions for the Twenty-First Century

Spiritual Questions for the Twenty-First Century

Essays in Honor of Joan D. Chittister

Edited by
Mary Hembrow Snyder

ORBIS BOOKS

Maryknoll, New York 10545

Fifth printing, October 2002

The Catholic Foreign Mission Society of America (Maryknoll) recruits and trains people for overseas missionary service. Through Orbis Books, Maryknoll aims to foster the international dialogue that is essential to mission. The books published, however, reflect the opinions of their authors and are not meant to represent the official position of the Society.

To obtain more information about Maryknoll and Orbis Books, please visit our website at www.maryknoll.org.

Library of Congress Cataloging-in-Publication Data
Spiritual questions for the twenty-first century : essays in honor of Joan D. Chittister / edited by Mary Hembrow Snyder.
    p. cm.
  ISBN 1-57075-369-5 (pbk.)
  1. Spirituality – Catholic Church. I. Chittister, Joan. II. Snyder, Mary Hembrow.

  BX2350.65 .S63 2001
  282'.01'12 – dc21

00-049163

Contents

Part II
BUILDING COMMUNITY:
THE ECCLESIAL CHALLENGE

Part III
TRANSFORMING STRUCTURES:
THE GLOBAL CHALLENGE

Preface

The subject of this *Festschrift* is not Joan Chittister! She refused to allow that when we initially discussed this project. Typical Joan — she wanted the scope and content of any tribute to her to engage as wide an audience as possible. Thus we chose the area that best encompasses her life's work, namely, contemporary spirituality. Our twin hopes for this book, then, are that it, first of all, provoke, nurture, and encourage all people seriously seeking, in Joan's words, deeper "consciousness of the sacred." Secondly, we hope that this book will underscore the inescapable connection that exists between such consciousness and "action on behalf of justice" for the least among us, including our endangered Earth.

Moreover, having the courage to question every aspect of her life's journey is undoubtedly one of the defining characteristics of this deeply spiritual, deeply Catholic, deeply Benedictine woman. It therefore seemed most appropriate to weave a *Festschrift* for Joan around the theme of questioning. Consequently, we asked each contributor to address this: "What do you think is the most important spiritual question of our time?" The diversity and richness of the responses illuminate the darkness that has become so representative of the times in which we are living.

For example, Ivone Gebara wonders why we human beings lack the confidence we need in each other to create a truly just and peaceful world; Diarmuid O'Murchu suggests that we must expand our horizons of meaning; Elizabeth Johnson proposes that the question of right relationship with the Earth encompasses all the other significant spiritual and ethical questions of our time; Tissa Balasuriya raises the question of global apartheid caused by unjust land distribution among the races as singularly pressing.

As the editor, I conceived this *Festschrift* to pay homage to a woman who has been a prophetic voice in the Catholic church for over three decades. I believe Joan deserves this tribute. I hope it will always be a reminder to her that what she has dared to risk on behalf of "Christ, gospel, people, community and commitment rooted in love" has made all the difference for so very many of us.

Acknowledgments

For the sabbatical that made this book possible, I thank Dr. William P. Garvey, President of Mercyhurst College, and Dr. Joseph F. Gower, Vice-President for Academic Affairs;

For the generous support of my colleagues and friends at Mercyhurst College, I thank Catherine Anderson, Alice Edwards, Thomas Forsthoefel, Heidi Hosey, David Livingston, Lisa Mary McCartney, RSM, Joanne McGurk, Kevin Sullivan, Sr. Mary Eustace Taylor, RSM, Carol Ann Voltz, RSM, Mary Jeanne Weiser, and most especially, Dorothy Stoner, OSB;

For those who critiqued the manuscript, allowed me to interview them, or otherwise gave me help in myriad ways, I thank Stephanie Campbell, OSB, Mary Lee Farrell, GNSH, Margaret Mary Kraus, OSB, Mary Lou Kownacki, OSB, Judge George Levin, Catherine Manning, SSJ, Rita Mary Olszewski, RSM, Sara Pitzer, Janet Staub, OSB, Kathleen Stephens, Mary Louise St. John, OSB, and Maureen Tobin, OSB. Special mention goes to Marlene Bertke, OSB, who generously read this multiple times and whose editing advice was invaluable;

For the faithful friends whose "random acts of kindness" meant so much as I worked to complete this project, I thank Jo Clark, Ann Daugherty, Therese Forsthoefel, Sharon Heiser, Deb King, Cindy Liotta, and Nancy Sabol;

To each of the contributors to this *Festschrift* — their humility gave me pause, and their resilience was refreshing;

To my enthusiastic, patient, and gifted editor, Robert Ellsberg, and Catherine Costello, whose meticulous editing skills made this book publication-ready;

To the woods I live in where I wrote this book — for all this sacred place and its inhabitants taught me about change, growth, risk, death, and new life;

To my precious dog, Rosie — for the inexplicable joy and comfort she gave me;

To Joan herself, who has so richly revealed the face of the Divine to us;

And finally, to June C. Pintea, Curt Cadorette, and William J. Kowalski — friends rich in wisdom and compassion who illumined the way....

My deep gratitude to all.

Introduction

She who reconciles the ill-matched threads
Of her life, and weaves them gratefully
Into a single cloth —
It's she who drives the loudmouths from the hall
And clears it for a different celebration

Where the one guest is you.
In the softness of evening
It's you she receives.

You are the partner of her loneliness,
The unspeaking center of her monologues.
With each disclosure you encompass more
And she stretches beyond what limits her,
To hold you.[1]

Have you ever wondered what the "Energy of God" might look like embodied in a human being? I have — it looks like Joan Daugherty Chittister!

Whether you agree or disagree with her, you cannot deny that experiencing her energy stimulates some kind of response. I believe this is what happens when we come into the presence (whether personally or through the written word) of someone intimately connected to the Holy Mystery. Then, like the hemorrhaging woman or the rich young man, we are provoked at our core and must respond.

For thirty-five years the Energy of God has found a home in Joan D. Chittister. For thirty-five years she has obediently surrendered to that Energy, passionately interacted with that Energy, creatively offered to share that Energy with any bold enough to engage it.

As a result, monasticism in particular and religious life in general are forever altered; our blindness to the injustice women experience in the church and larger world is forever altered; our ability to ignore the cries of poor, inner-city children is forever altered; our naïveté about ecclesiastical and foreign policies that oppress is forever altered; our discomfort with those whose religious heritage is different from ours is forever altered; our inhospitality to the stranger, be she or he gay,

13

physically challenged, or a refugee from Central America, is forever altered; our struggle to trust our own experience of the Holy One is forever altered; our confusion about how to create a contemplative life in the service of peace and justice is forever altered.

Most importantly, I wonder if Joan's greatest contribution to her own church and to people of faith everywhere isn't this: she inspires us to honor our own questions and to trust that it is the Energy of God that gives them birth.

I wonder further. Could it also be that, retrospectively speaking, questions have had the power to propel Joan because they arose from "the ill-matched threads," the trajectory of contradictions that have circumscribed her life and that consequently were befriended by the grace of the Energy of God that so describes who she has become?

From Home to Community

By the time she was in the third grade, Joan Chittister admits, "the ability to hold opposites in tension became a practiced skill."[2] She had learned at a very early age how sobering life's contradictions can be. She also learned to weave boldly the "ill-matched threads" they fashioned, unapologetically so.

Joan's mother, Loretta Cuneo Daugherty Chittister, dreamed of entering the convent as a young girl in the early 1930s. She had, in fact, secretly sewn a cache of convent clothes that she had hidden under her bed. But this youngest of thirteen children was needed at home to help care for her dying father. Entering a convent was out of the question. When Joan's grandmother discovered Loretta's convent wardrobe, the dream died.

> The image of her finding and destroying my mother's convent clothes put a lump in my young throat that stayed there forever. I knew that the telling of the story was meant to say that my mother would never do the same thing to me, that what I wanted to do in life she would never stop. But no matter how hard I tried I could never lift the burden of dreams surrendered, either from my mother's shoulders or from my own.[3]

Had Joan's mother been the youngest boy child desiring to enter the priesthood, would he have had to surrender his dream? One can only hazard a guess: it is unlikely. Women then were expected to forgo their dreams in a way men were not. Joan never forgot this.

Loretta Cuneo married Dan Daugherty instead. She was nineteen, he twenty-one. Joan was born in 1936. By 1938, Loretta's second dream was denied her: Dan died unexpectedly. Now she faced enormous loss, coupled with the threat of poverty and sole responsibility for Joan. As she tells it, the contradiction borne by her father's untimely death resulted in Joan's vocation.

Two Sisters of Mercy from the local parish convent offered their compassionate presence to the family as they sat prayerfully near the casket. Loretta told Joan that the sisters were friends of her daddy and friends of God whose responsibility it was "to give the souls of little girls' daddies to God."[4] Joan was captivated by this explanation and determined one day to do the same thing for someone else.[5]

A year and a half later, Loretta married Harold "Dutch" Chittister, who adopted Joan. He was a good, honest, hardworking man, but he was Protestant. Such a "mixed marriage" was frowned upon, but this Irish, Catholic, single mother, struggling financially to clothe and feed young Joan, had no other options.

> Years later, when it was clear not only that the marriage had broken down but had, in fact, never really been good, I asked her why she had married him in the first place. The answer was always the same: "I married Dutch Chittister to give you a home," she said over and over. "There was nothing else a woman could do." The answer seared then and only burned more deeply over the years: there was nothing else a woman could do. I have never been able to get that answer out of my mind.[6]

Loretta did not have a high school education. As skilled a seamstress as she was, such work was not adequately remunerative when raising a child alone. Compelled by circumstances to marry, Joan's mother culled from her own suffering a dictum that she firmly planted in her daughter: "You can do anything you put your mind to."[7] While it contradicted her own life experience, it became a foundational principle upon which Joan Chittister built her life.

Like any Catholic child of the time, Joan learned not to question her faith, at least in public. Yet she struggled with the religious imperialism that dogmatically proclaimed, "Only Catholics go to heaven." "How could a loving God have favorites?" she wondered. Her experience of family members who were faithful religious persons, albeit Protestant, contradicted what she had been taught. Her father's anger at the arrogance of the Catholic worldview grew in direct proportion to the diminishment he felt for being a Presbyterian in a largely Catholic culture.

He chided Joan's mother for sending her to Catholic schools and criticized Joan for becoming increasingly devoted to her religion. The sisters who taught Joan had an enormous impact on her life. They were role models, offering her an alternative way of being a woman at a time when alternatives were few. She had choices her mother did not. And she realized this by the time she was ten years old.

Originally from Dubois, Pennsylvania, she and her family moved to Erie, Pennsylvania, when Joan was in the fourth grade — to the east side. There was diversity in this working-class neighborhood, but they were poor and Joan knew it. Without calling it "classism," she was aware, as any working-class child with a sensitive intelligence is aware, that she lived "on the wrong side of the tracks." She writes, "Every morning I walked down Peach Street, under the railroad trestle, past the railroad station, beyond the park, to the world, to school and the Catholic upper-class. Every night I walked back up Peach Street to the poor. And nothing ever brought the two worlds together, except church and the image of an upper-class Jesus consorting with lepers."[8] Political and theological contradictions were not lost on this gifted little girl. She would expose them the rest of her life.

Perhaps the most compelling contradiction of Joan's life, however, is that she became a woman religious at all.

Because of her mother's financial resourcefulness, as well as Joan's willingness to work multiple jobs after school, she attended a Catholic high school, St. Benedict's Academy. Her father disapproved. Nonetheless, there she flourished and realized what she wanted to do with her life. She relates, "Someplace very early in the year, I announced to my mother while we did the dishes together that this was the convent I would be entering. Here kids were people and life was full of joy. 'Take your time,' she said. 'Be sure.' But I was already sure."[9]

High school was a wonderful experience of camaraderie and community for her. Clubs, parties, dances, sports, and study engaged her on every level. "I'd never been so happy. All the child in me that had been lost for years seemed to emerge at once," she writes.[10] Journalism became her concentration by way of default when she incurred a sports injury during a volleyball game. Not only did she become editor of the newspaper, but president of her class as well. When her involvement in school activities competed with the extracurricular employment she had, the sisters gave her two scholarships that included free lunches, as well as free tuition.

At the same time, larger world events did not impinge on her consciousness, politically speaking. While Hitler's atrocities were exposed, while McCarthyism plagued the country, while Eisenhower and Nixon governed, while the official church applauded the U.S. war effort in Korea and became obsessed with the conversion of Russia, Joan's high school world remained unsullied by it all. "Politics and economics and patriarchy had nothing to do with us."[11]

Nevertheless, she did have encounters with sexism as an adolescent girl that jolted her awareness that something was seriously amiss between the sexes. As she sold the school newspaper in the cafeteria of the local boys' high school, she became angry and dismayed by their disrespect and disdain, especially when the male teachers did nothing to discourage such behavior. Once, her mother had remarked to her, "Men always think they own you."[12] But Joan wasn't about to be owned by anyone, and these experiences of the opposite sex ignited, like a slow-but-sure burning flame, the incipient feminist consciousness that was to become a hallmark of her commitment to justice for women.

Poetry and literature absorbed her. She was enthralled by Sister Madeleva, Gerard Manley Hopkins, Frances Thompson, J. F. Powers, G. K. Chesterton, and Galsworthy. They became her "spiritual directors." She wanted to be like them and make a similarly substantial contribution to the world. Her religious sensibilities ripened to the point where she decided she was ready to pursue her vocation. Joan, at this time, was only a sophomore in high school. No community would have her.

Guileless and undaunted, she rang the bell of the prioress of the Benedictine community and told her she wanted to enter the convent. Mother Sylvester asked her how old she was and when Joan replied, "Fifteen," she told her that sixteen was the minimum age for entering the convent and sent her on her way.[13]

Joan was undeterred. The next year, when she turned sixteen, Joan went back to Mother Sylvester. But she discouraged her from entering because of her age and because Joan was an only child. Two days later Joan returned with her mother to convince the prioress that, indeed, Joan's mother supported her desire. Her sense of urgency allowed no compromise. Finally, all three agreed: Joan would enter the Benedictine Sisters of Erie on September 8, 1952, despite her father's disapproval. Five weeks later, in mid-October, Joan Chittister was stricken with polio.

> The whole question was, "Would they keep me?" I didn't walk for four ye`ars. I was in a wheelchair and a long leg brace and an iron lung, and when I think back, the community must have had just a terrible time trying to determine whether or not in

conscience they could keep this kid that they weren't sure could ever really live the life and who would always be, at best, an exception. And they kept me. And I'll tell you, people may look now and say, "What has happened to the Erie Benedictines, have they gone crazy?" And I would say that if you had looked back at 1952 and seen how they dealt with the poor and disenfranchised then, in the person of Joan Chittister, you should have had fair warning about who this group was.[14]

And, it was fair warning about who this intrepid, tenacious, and daring young woman might become with the appropriate mentoring, opportunities, and intellectual/spiritual challenges. The subprioress at that time, Sister Theophane, also the academy principal and community nurse, was wise enough to recognize the exceptional woman Joan could become. She oversaw the exercises Joan had to perform to enhance the development of her muscles wasted by polio. At the same time, she listened to Joan's questions and nurtured her intellectual and spiritual hungers in ways uncommon then to the formation of young sisters. Sr. Theophane gave her Merton, Marmion, and Teresa of Avila to read, along with a journal. Joan, aching to be challenged more substantially, began to feel again that there was hope that both she and the community "dwelt in possibility" — a possibility Joan would one day be called upon to embody.

From Law to Conscience

Another "ill-matched thread" of her life that Joan reconciled in the face of great anguish and turmoil was the stark truth that by the end of the 1960s, she wanted to leave the community. This was an enormous turnaround for a woman who had once declared, "I have never, even in the early grades, felt called to anything but the religious life."

Joan, like many other women religious at that time, felt betrayed by the cauldron of change and renewal occasioned by the Second Vatican Council. The old absolutes were gone. Governance, community life, ministry, formation, prayer, liturgy, even the vows — all were called into question as the council directed religious communities to rediscover the charism of their founders so as to be able to recognize and respond to the signs of the times.

Looking back, she describes herself as "a perfect example of the unthinking conservative."

> I bought it all, meaning I never confronted it intellectually. I loved the community, I loved its spirit, I loved its members. Even in 1952 I thought that a lot of stuff we did was (a) groundless, (b) meaningless, (c) silly — all of the above, some of the above, none of the above. But I never questioned it.... The point is that no matter what the public image is, I did not lead renewal. I'd *love* to be able to say I did, but I really didn't. I feared it.... I came to renewal slowly.[15]

There was, however, no place to hide. One way or another the contradictions that renewal exposed and the questions it provoked about the meaning and purpose of religious life demanded scrutiny. For Joan personally, for religious life in particular, and for the church in general, this demanded a fundamentally different self-understanding.

Her parents were poignantly instructive. While they clearly indicated they would support whatever decision she made, they also urged her to examine two things: the impact her leaving would have on the community and her understanding of commitment. By taking their wise counsel she began to filter the accidentals from the essentials and for her, "the distinguishing principle became love."[16]

> You just finally had to get to the point where you said, What really matters? Is it a veil that matters? Is it a skirt that matters? Is it a ministry that matters? What matters? And when it came right down to it, the only answer I could come up with was that Christ mattered, gospel mattered, and people mattered, and that was it. So I just decided to go for those three.[17]

Christ. Gospel. People. Community and commitment rooted in love. Having reassessed and reconfigured the foundations of her vocation, Joan threw herself into the maelstrom of contradictions raised by the turmoil of the times. Of this and only this was she certain: she would never be the same, her community would never be the same, the institutional church would never be the same. Neither would Erie, Pennsylvania, the U.S.A., or the global community. The stakes were soul-sized.

By 1968 she had an M.A. in communications from the University of Notre Dame. An electrifying English teacher, she captivated the high school students she taught with her energy, passion, and creativity. Between 1968 and 1971 she obtained a Ph.D. in communication theory and social psychology from Penn State. Joan was the first in her community to have a doctorate. While trying to finish it, she was elected a delegate to the chapter of the Federation of St. Scholastica, the largest group of Benedictine women in the United States. And, at the age of thirty-five she proceeded to become the youngest president of the federation ever elected. Two years before her second term in this position concluded, she was also elected president of American Benedictine Prioresses, a post she held from 1975 to 1990. It was most unusual to be elected to either of these prestigious positions without first having been a prioress. But at the national level her sisters recognized Joan's leadership ability, as did the Leadership Conference of Women Religious, which also elected her its president in 1976. Her peers in leadership saw her as a woman unafraid "to speak truth to power" on the salient issues that concerned not only monastic and religious life, but also that of the larger church.

In all three leadership positions Joan helped dismantle the myth that equated being contemplative with "fleeing the world." She was a living witness that monastic spirituality was nondualistic. Consequently, she gave Benedictine women in particular a larger, deeper sense of their own identity. As a former student and friend of forty years, Kathy Stephens remarked, "If you don't understand what it means to be a Benedictine then you can't understand Joan." In a phrase, it means "one who listens." In Joan's vision this meant listening to four realities: "the Gospels, the Rule, one another and the world."[18] Out of this deep listening she would later develop a profound contribution to contemporary spirituality. In the meantime she helped all women religious, in monastic and apostolic communities both, to name their common oppressor: patriarchy.

Elected prioress of her own community in 1978, she galvanized her sisters to meet the needed liturgical renewal head-on, as Benedictine *women.* Inclusive language was adopted in the Liturgy of the Hours and feminine expression of the Divine encouraged in the planning of eucharistic celebrations. Liturgical life became more creative, more artistic. It prayerfully reflected the gifts of the sisters, both mind and body, in a way never before actualized.

By this time Joan was a highly sought-after writer, lecturer, and consultant to religious communities. She saw no contradiction between the questions behind the renewal of religious life — questions about values, identity, meaning, authority — and the questions facing the larger world. She believed that women and men religious in particular, and all Christians in general, must be "leavens of justice" if they were to be faithful to Jesus' vision of the reign of God.

In an intracommunity publication she initiated during her first term as prioress, Joan wrote, "We have to ask ourselves what we really do for the good of this world; what our use of things says to others; is the sign we give authentic?"[19]

Under her nurturing direction, and building upon the legacy of her predecessor, Sister Mary Margaret Kraus, Joan encouraged the growth of her sisters and the commitment of the community to the issues/questions of the day. She created a climate within the community that fostered personal development. Her sisters felt free to dream new dreams. Dialogue and reflection took place around issues such as assertiveness, stress management, conflict resolution, interpersonal relationships, emotional maturity, pluralism, and diversity. She challenged her sisters by asking them, "What do you know least about but realize you should understand better if you are to advance in religious and community life?"[20] While encouraging the personal growth of each of her sisters, she also made possible the expanding sense of ministry demanded by the needs of the people of God.

During Joan's first year as prioress the community embraced a corporate commitment that had a decidedly sociopolitical expression, but that was rooted in the monastic tradition. Prior to the Second Vatican Council the community's institutional commitment was predominantly in the area of education. Renewal had brought opportunities for the sisters to rethink their ministries. At the same time, renewal had the potential to undermine the common sense of identity and purpose the sisters enjoyed when their ministry was primarily education related. The genius of the corporate commitment was that it gave them a renewed sense of focus and cohesion, a unified sense of direction, as they continued to rediscover and creatively express the Benedictine charism. Thus, no matter what work each sister was doing, she aligned herself with the corporate commitment. And that commitment became the community's prophetic response to a single justice issue. It was the community's way of taking seriously and concretely Catholic social teaching. It was the community's radical commitment to Jesus' vision of the reign of God. It was a commitment that Erie Benedictines knew would put them at risk for "being out of step" with the conventional wisdom of the day, namely, the societal and ecclesiastical norms that contradicted gospel values.

Initially, the corporate commitment focused on nuclear disarmament. Since 1974 it has been reviewed every four years and today reads, "to model the Benedictine charism of peace by working for disarmament, ecological stewardship and social justice in solidarity with the poor and oppressed, especially women."

The corporate commitment was issued because Joan, as prioress, had the vision to initiate it, and because her sisters had the vision and courage to articulate its prophetic witness. No dualism here between monastic life and the secular world. On the contrary, such a vision is a boldly Benedictine gesture, a stark reminder of how Benedictines express their search for God.

> Vision is not physical. It is a quality of the soul. People with vision hone in, laser-like, to the presence of God in life. They see the holy, bleeding, suffering, feuding world as God sees the world: as one and as sacred. In love with a loving God, they are impelled to love God's world as God does.... They stretch beyond the demands of the personal, the chauvinistic, the nationalistic, the sectarian, even the doctrinal, to do the will of God for the entire world. They are not trapped by the pitiful little agendas of color or gender or hierarchy or place. They live possessed by the will of God for the world and spend themselves for its coming.[21]

Here is vintage Joan, "driving the loudmouths from the hall," those perpetrators of militarism, sexism, racism, classism, homophobia. In solidarity with her is her community. Together they prepare for "a different celebration," where all the excluded are now the guests, where all the denigrated are now welcome. "Come right in and disturb our perfect lives. You are the Christ for us today."[22]

As vision became reality, the guests were served. Under Joan's leadership the community created a housing ministry to middle- and lower-income elderly and physically challenged persons through the management of the Benetwood Apartments. Joan was also instrumental in making the monastery grounds a place that addressed the spiritual hunger of lay people and clergy. It was her dream to construct hermitages on their property to give access to solitude, silence, and participation in the rhythm of monastic life to anyone as needed. Persons from all over the country and world have been refreshed and renewed because of her dream.

In addition, during Joan's tenure as prioress the community sponsored the Second Harvest Food Bank, thereby providing food to the hungry of northwestern Pennsylvania. It closed its four-year academy for girls due to a decrease in enrollment occasioned by the presence in Erie at that time of three secondary schools for young women. Its limited population could no longer sustain them all. St. Benedict's Academy had served the east side of Erie for 118 years. In its place the community recreated a ministry of education offering the most disenfranchised in the city opportunities to empower themselves and their children through self-development and employment skills. Simultaneously, the community under Joan endorsed the Sanctuary Movement and became a place of refuge for those fleeing the oppression in El Salvador and Guatemala.

While this is not an exhaustive list of the ministries sponsored by the community throughout Joan's three terms as prioress, it is a poignant glimpse into the "action on behalf of justice" that occurred under her direction. Both she and the community were severely criticized for their countercultural stance — a price they willingly paid for being an unambiguous embodiment of the compassionate, liberating Christ in today's world. For this "unthinking conservative" heretofore immersed in order, regularity, rule, and strict obedience, the journey to conscience, to honoring questions as well as experience, was rugged and relentless. But the integrity of her personal search was matched by the integrity of her community and their uncommon commitment to those most marginalized at home and abroad. The contradictions would not, could not, always be reconciled, the questions not always resolved. But Joan accepted this, as did her sisters. After all, "the Rule is clear: love costs."[23]

From Prioress to Prophet

After twelve years in office Joan concluded her ministry as prioress in 1990. It had become obvious by then to many who really knew her that she needed to give her gifts to the universal church and to build her agenda around the issues it faced globally. In service to that calling, she began to write and speak prolifically. During the last decade she has penned more than twenty books, given nearly thirty keynote addresses or conferences in the U.S. and abroad, contributed chapters to twenty books edited by others, written over one hundred articles for various newspapers and periodicals, traveled to South Africa, England, Australia, Ireland, Italy, China, the Philippines, Hungary, Russia, Austria, and Israel, held ten educational positions as a writer-in-residence or invited fellow, and received numerous awards that include nine honorary doctorates from Catholic institutions.

Perhaps one of her most treasured accomplishments is the collaborative vision she shared with Sister Mary Lou Kownacki, OSB, and many generous people in the city of Erie to give birth to the Neighborhood Art House. A ministry of the community located in the inner city, the purpose of the Neighborhood Art House is to provide year-round free lessons in art, music, dance, and literature to over six hundred poor children in that city. It was begun in 1994 because the

Benedictine Sisters of Erie "believe that the need for the arts in the lives of the poor is as real as their need for bread."

At the same time, this past decade of Joan's life found her becoming increasingly a global voice for justice, especially justice for women. She attended the Fourth World Conference on Women in China in 1995 and then traveled with the Peace Train Delegation, which visited forty-two countries from Helsinki to Beijing. She was one of only 230 women chosen to participate in this.

In 1999 she also attended the Parliament of World Religions in Cape Town, South Africa, where her voice, vision, and "listening ear" played a significant role in shaping a more human and holy world order.

All of these experiences have empowered Joan to make one of the most influential contributions to contemporary spirituality in the latter part of the twentieth century. In a singular way she has taken the gospel message, the Rule of St. Benedict, the insights of others, and the experience of those who suffer most from injustice in our world and issued a hope-filled remedy for what ails us at the turn of the twenty-first century: be converted and become a contemplative! One day at a time, albeit for a lifetime, dare to embrace conversion. One day at a time, albeit for a lifetime, dare to become a woman or a man of prayer. One day at a time, albeit for a lifetime, you will then "have the vision to do every day whatever must be done to make God present in this place, at this time, whatever the cost."[24]

Joan's unique interpretation of what conversion and contemplation mean today has captured the spiritual and moral imagination of God-seekers across denominational lines. Why? Because people find her passion contagious and her message authentic. Because people know in their heart of hearts that both conversion and contemplation are keys to dealing with the difficulties of an age gone mad with self-indulgence and diffidence toward the poor. Because her message offers an alternative to the legacy of the violence we cannot eradicate simply by building more prisons. Because her words release in all people of goodwill radical hope in themselves and their communities in a period of diminishing, sometimes dark, expectations.

The spirituality Joan offers to the world is an engaged spirituality. She teaches that if individually and collectively we can transform this behemoth called injustice, then we will recognize the right of every woman to be fully human, the right of every child to a safe environment, the right of every poor human being to a dignified life. Then and only then will we turn our swords into plowshares and our spears into pruning hooks; then and only then will we refuse the anthropocentrism that threatens the annihilation of this planet. Be converted and become a contemplative, she urges us, for

> The answer never changes. In every great religious tradition the concept is clear. To be contemplative we must become converted to the consciousness that makes us one with the universe, in tune with the cosmic voice of God. We must become aware of the sacred in every single element of life. We must bring beauty to birth in a poor and plastic world. We must restore the human community. We must grow in concert with the God who is within. We must be healers in a harsh society.[25]

Despite the agnosticism, the narcissism, the cynicism of our age, Joan Chittister invites us to seek both the God within and the God of the cosmos. She invites us to heal the pain within and the pain of the earthworld. She invites us to entertain our deepest and most extravagant longings for communion with each other, creation, and the Divine — despite the agnosticism, the narcissism, the cynicism of our age.

So, in the final analysis, "What manner of woman is this?" What drives her, most fundamentally, to "live the questions," to embrace the contradictions, to reconcile "the ill-matched threads" she has encountered everywhere she has turned? Why her "breathless impatience with injustice," her "deep sensitivity to evil?"[26] Why do her words propel us ineluctably into the truth of our accountability for the least among us?

What drives her is both simply and profoundly this: *her love affair with the Divine.* It is her intimate, joyous, bewildering, sometimes dark and painful seeking of the Holy One that, when all is said and done, dynamically upholds the center and ground of her being. It is the extravagant hospitality she offered to this Ultimate of Guests, expressed in nearly fifty years of monastic life, that made this Guest "the partner of her loneliness" and "the unspeaking center of her monologues." It was the unrelenting hunger for *this* relationship that brooked no obstacle to communion in the course of her life. It was the endless passion for *this* relationship that thrust her into positions of leadership that asked more of her than she ever dreamed she could give. It was the all-consuming desire for *this* relationship that fueled her bold, courageous articulation of the questions — questions about our images of God, about personal and social sin, about war, militarism, racism, classism, and ecocide, about violence against poor children, gay people, and the elderly, about the horrendous and unnecessary suffering of the people of Central America, South Africa, and Haiti, about a patriarchal church, society, and world that denied women the right to be fully human, about whether or not it was truly possible for a *conscious* woman to remain Catholic at all.

Time and again she found herself confronting the powers and principalities. She refused to be compromised or silenced. The contradictions, the questions, the ill-matched threads combined over time to provoke her to "prophetic utterance." And "prophetic utterance is rarely cryptic . . . it is urging, alarming, forcing onward, as if the words gushed forth from the heart of God, seeking entrance to the heart and mind of man carrying a summons as well as an involvement . . . the language is luminous and explosive, firm and contingent, harsh and compassionate, a fusion of contradictions."[27] Summoned by the One Who Would Be Heard, Joan Chittister could not refuse what decades of faithful seeking had done to her, namely, empowered her "to listen with the ear of her heart." In her own words, "When we start listening to the Word of God, to others around us, to those with wise hearts and tried souls, life changes from the dry and the independent to the compassionate and meaningful. When we start listening to the Word of God, people have a right to expect something new of us."[28] Abraham Heschel confirms that "the prophet's ear is inclined to God." Moreover, "this is the marvel of a prophet's work," namely, that in the prophet's words *the invisible God becomes audible.*"[29]

Thus, I wonder.

I wonder again and again: "What manner of woman is this?"

Prophet, oh yes. Visionary, no question. Gifted teacher, absolutely. Friend to the forgotten ones, clearly. Fully human being, undoubtedly! One who listens deeply. One who honors the contradictions. One who pursues the questions. One who is always stretching "beyond what limits her, / To hold you." And your reign.

For us.

Weaving.

Gratefully weaving.

One single cloth.

Mary Hembrow Snyder
May 15, 2000

Notes

1. *Rilke's Book of Hours: Love Poems to God,* trans. Anita Barrows and Joanna Macy (New York: Riverhead Books, 1997), 64.

2. Joan Chittister, unpublished manuscript, 1986, 5.

3. Ibid., 2.

4. Ibid., 3.

5. Ibid.

6. Ibid., 4.

7. Ibid., 6.

8. Ibid., 11.

9. Ibid., 13.

10. Ibid.

11. Ibid., 14.

12. Ibid., 15.

13. Ibid., 16.

14. Joan Chittister, "Sister Says," in *Once a Catholic,* ed. Peter Occhiogrosso (New York: Ballantine Books, 1987), 9.

15. Ibid., 12.

16. Ibid., 13.

17. Ibid.

18. Joan Chittister, *Wisdom Distilled from the Daily: Living the Rule of St. Benedict Today* (San Francisco: HarperCollins, 1990), 15.

19. Joan Chittister, *The Leaven* 2, no. 3 (February 1980).

20. Joan Chittister, *The Leaven* 3, no. 2 (January 1981).

21. Joan Chittister, *Illuminated Life: Monastic Wisdom for Seekers of Light* (Maryknoll, N.Y.: Orbis Books, 2000), 118–19.

22. Joan Chittister, *The Rule of St. Benedict: Insights for the Ages* (New York: Crossroad, 1992), 141.

23. Chittister, *Wisdom Distilled from the Daily,* 41.

24. Chittister, *Illuminated Life,* 120.

25. Ibid., 81.

26. Abraham J. Heschel, *The Prophets: An Introduction* (New York: Harper and Row, 1969), 4.

27. Ibid., 6–7.

28. Chittister, *Wisdom Distilled from the Daily,* 20.

29. Heschel, *The Prophets,* 20–21.

Part I

Nurturing Consciousness

The Personal Challenge

1

Equilibrium

Daniel Berrigan, SJ

Equilibrium —
favored word of mystics;
equilibrium
in all save love.

A high-wire act, one foot firm,
one in midair;
brief, dangerous;
          a land
creature essaying
adverse elements.

Some few are skilled
breathtakingly.
          They run
that equator, as though riding
a burning arrow.
          (In all things
knowledgeable, above all
in love.)

Regard not only
the arrow, but the gradual
spent force of the string
let go.
          How graceful
the bow at rest;

          but
O under pressure, like
the bold breath
of Creator Spirit. Twang!
And torn
from thin air, a song of songs!

2

Better to Love Than to Fade Away

Gail Grossman Freyne

Prologue

Yes, I tell you again, it is easier for a camel to pass through the eye of a needle than for a rich person to enter the kingdom of God. (Matt. 19:24)

The Story

The most important spiritual question of our time comes in the form of an answer: "If you want to be perfect, go home, sell all that you have, ... then come back and follow me" (Matt. 19:21). This author's reflex, in common with that of the rich young man and a long history of Christian response, was to consider this suggestion impossibly utopian, except for the chosen few. Yet, as announced by Jesus, it is a radical statement of human possibility for every one of us. But even to begin to approach the possibility of the possible, we need to reshape our understanding of what it means to be fully and inclusively human, radically so.

Matthew had a political axe to grind. He wanted the Jewish community to learn that keeping the law was not enough, for even if this was achieved, the essential question remained: "What more do I need to do?" The rich scion of a Jewish house, unlike his Greek counterpart, knew that perfection could not be achieved in isolation. From the prophetic tradition of Israel it is clear that perfection entailed the pursuit of justice, a virtue that could never be achieved by any legal code that was satisfied to list individual rights and the means to protect them. Personal virtue always remained an incomplete response in the face of collective sin. Thus, for the rich young man, perfection and justice were always essentially intertwined and entailed the demand for radical, social action. Matthew repeats Hosea's declaration of God's will: "It is mercy [in the sense of acts of love, care, and kindness] not sacrifice [in the sense of pious practices] that wins favor with me" (Matt. 12:7). In Third Isaiah we are told to refrain from judgment, "the pointing of the finger and speaking of wickedness" and instead to "pour yourself out for the afflicted" (Isa. 58:9–10). Love each other more than the law if you want to be beloved of God, we are told.

If we accept the ancient wisdom that perfection is not to be sought in isolation, then perhaps the meaning of the declaration to "go home" is also not as obvious as would first appear. Where do we really dwell? Out of a species history of approximately two hundred thousand years, we have stepped over at a frantic pace into that small segment of human existence, the third millennium of Christian time. The stunning explosion of human capacity at the turn of the last century — the telephone and radio waves, electric light and the car — quite literally put wings on our heels; we moved from Kitty Hawk to the moon in a mere sixty-six years. We also managed to slaughter, torture, and starve each other with greater efficiency; Einstein's formulation of $E=mc^2$ to the instant cremation of cities took us just forty-one years. The largest and most recent of our inventions, cyberspace, has saturated us with pornography. We have made a brave new world with which to distort and destroy ourselves, even making it possible for this species to preempt our planet's inherent movement toward disintegration. All of this is terrifying, especially for our children, because, while it is our legacy, it is their inheritance.

This "home" that we have constructed for ourselves is in the condition that it is because we have failed to understand the profound reality that human life, nonhuman life, and the entire ecosphere are intimately connected. Instead, we have accepted the Aristotelian notion that "different from" means "better than" and complacently located ourselves atop the hierarchical pyramid of the Great Chain of Being, refusing to recognize that humankind, being made of the same stuff as everything else in creation, is embedded within the natural world. With extraordinary hubris, we have constructed our social world at a dangerous distance from the context upon which we depend for our existence. The glare that blinds — bright lights on twinkling consoles — makes it nearly impossible for us to see that we are now more vulnerable than we have ever been, not just individually but as a species.

If we are ever to engage radically with the humanitarian and ethical vision of Jesus encapsulated within this story, we need to embrace a transformative understanding of the concepts of human embodiment and our embeddedness within the natural world. In terms of our embodied, intrahuman relations, the question of the rich young man recently has been posed in wickedly realistic terms: "How much of yourself can you express without endangering your affluence?"[1] The really wicked answer is, "Not much." Not much, unless we realize that all spirituality, without hint of paradox, must be corporeal. We need to examine our embodiment in all its manifestations and complexity. We can never flourish as a species until we acknowledge that the Other is as human as I: poor or rich, black or white, female or male, gay or straight, old or young. Reversing the order of expression of these familiar pairings is not once again to privilege the first named, but simply an attempt to begin to destabilize the traditional, and sometimes seemingly eradicable, hierarchically oppositional way in which they have been understood. Shifting the emphasis is going to cost us, not least of all, money. Providing housing for every person living in a shelter would play havoc with the city budget; welcoming more refugees than we could afford would be more than we could expend; paying women for the caring they do in immediate and extended families would swallow the cost of warheads; if gays and lesbians could marry, insurance companies would have to pay death benefits to the deceased's spouse; and if the elderly and retired were given pensions equivalent to state representatives, nobody would go into politics. Isaiah was a thoroughly modern man. Pouring ourselves out for the afflicted would really hurt.

In terms of our embeddedness within the natural world, the fragility of the human condition that we currently experience has been produced by two interlocking expressions of power, one emanating from science and the other in philosophy, the former more familiar than the latter. In the first instance, as I have already mentioned, we have developed the ability to destroy entire cities in an instant. Perhaps less fiendishly, but in the end just as thoroughly, we rape our natural heritage. Horror and fear have produced a dawning awareness that technique that lacks spirituality is the greatest tragedy of Western civilization. We respond, at the superficial level, with laws to protect the environment, reminiscent of the way we tinker with remedies for poverty. But both sets of laws emanate from an unexamined belief that to steward the earth or its poor is sufficient, a mindset that implies the same system can be continued by future generations. We want more of the same but for a little longer. Yet the self-regulating market economy which makes all of society subservient to its needs, dependent as it is upon natural resources and cheap labor, grinds on.

However, it is the second, philosophical expression of power that causes and provides the justification for the first. We have never adequately theorized the concept of nature and thus we have precluded the possibility of comprehending what it might mean to be, and therefore to become, fully or more inclusively human. We have been used to thinking that the more we distance ourselves from nature, the more rational we are, the more human we become. But this is a view of humanity that has been constructed by men, in opposition to, and by exclusion of, both women and nature. The forms of embodiment that are particular to women — giving birth, lactating, mothering, and the necessary daily tasks of life — are simultaneously considered natural and inferior to the rational activities of the public sphere of government and production. This traditional split of gender stereotypes has undergone some modifications, but it still represents much of the dynamic that underpins relationships between the sexes. Within such an understanding the human becomes a normative rather than a gender-neutral concept. It is, both in theory and in fact, a masculine model of humanity.

Until recently, women have sought equality by attempting to distance themselves from their traditional connection with "nature" by insinuating themselves within this masculine model. Such a solution must be inadequate, as women would do no more than embrace a model of humanity that had been instructed in their absence. Alternatively, deep ecologists have suggested that we must adopt an ecocentric ethic, espousing the total intermingling of person and planet. But this does not allow for any coherent theorizing of the distinctively human characteristic of self-consciousness that enables us to reshape our worlds and engage in moral reasoning. However, rather than eschew nature or attempt to collapse ourselves into it, what is required is a continuing analysis of the concept itself. Only such an exercise will allow for the rethinking of the traditional connection of the concepts of "women" and "nature," which will in turn permit a construction of an inclusive, or more perfectable and inclusive, understanding of "human-nature" in which men might also participate. Only such an exercise can provide the necessary foundation on which we can begin to build social justice and come "home" to ourselves as but one part of creation. Only such an exercise will set the parameters within which we can begin to think about "Sell all that you have, then come back and follow me."

How, precisely, to follow the ethical pronouncement of Jesus is the heart of the problem. We must choose: either "endanger our affluence" or return to the passivity of impotence. Yet, we are in a real dilemma, constantly suffering a collective identity crisis, always aware of the tensions, both logical and practical, between the particular and the general. At the personal level we feel as impotent as the rich young man, caught up as we are in our own heritage of the Enlightenment ideals of freedom and autonomy that justify a rampant individualism. Simultaneously, we comfort ourselves with the thought that we progress, hand in hand as one global village, toward some technically glorious Final Solution. But at the national level, where effective power is presumed to reside, treasurers remind us that the tentacles of corporatism wrap the globe and cannot be cut without causing chaos within the international monetary system; even governments appear unable to attempt a radical redistribution of wealth. We are riding a juggernaut to nowhere, we know it, and we cannot stop it. Yet we do try. There are endless initiatives: the United Nations, the Red Cross, Oxfam, Greenpeace, Amnesty International, to name but a few. What our children know, and we cannot deny, is that these organizations can only ameliorate the mess, not eradicate it. The fact of Isaiah's pronouncement makes it painfully clear that things were just as bad then, at least in relative terms, as they are now; *plus ça change, plus c'est la même chose* (the more things change, the more they remain the same).

The ethical vision of Jesus provides one answer for humanity that denies despair: if the problem is global then the solution must be local. "Follow me," he says. Not much of an answer, but it is all we have. As a psychotherapist I have learned the implications of this statement that change cannot be geared toward an impossible utopia but rather to the relief of present suffering. In his poem *Ithaka,* Constantinos Cavafy advises seafarers to make the journey a long one and to be old when they arrive at the island, for it is the island that gives us the reason to journey; without it we would never set out. Our greatest error is to define utopia as a practical possibility, for if we pursue what we can never achieve, we make it impossible to realize what is within our grasp. We have misunderstood the story of the rich young man to mean that Jesus was simply repeating the dictum of Isaiah: if you divest yourselves of wealth, "pour yourself out for the afflicted," all will somehow be perfect and just. Strange, really, because if we give up our money, we give up the power to make things happen. It is therefore the second half of Jesus' dictum — to follow him — that produces radical possibilities, for the more possible something becomes, the greater the likelihood of radical consequences.

To follow him means finding something for which it is worth laying down our lives — *on a daily basis.* Yes, in the first instance, those who have acquired wealth in the current mass madness are responsible for the suffering of those who have not. But it is not just money that we have to hand over; it is our selves, our safety, our security, our comfortable compliance, and our complicity. When we turn to individual therapy or religion in community, we are looking for meaning and a purpose worth living for. Every problem we have is a failure to love or be loved, and we know the part we play in both. The passivity of impotence is a failure to love; it is the paralysis that comes from too much autonomy. Yes, the world is a mess, we are engaged in a frenzy of destruction, injustice is everywhere, and I cannot fix it all; but I can do what I can do. Each of us must find what we love and give ourselves to it, with the support of like-minded others. This we must do without compromise, for this is what we have, indeed this is all that we have, to pass on to make the world a better place. Every time that we take up this challenge, we live; every time that we turn away, like the rich young man, we fade a little. He was only a recent inquisitor, but the answer he received remains the most important spiritual question of our time, of any time. Our task is to do something, to count for something, whether we are ever remembered for it or not. Putting on our sandals might be a good beginning.

Epilogue

While doing up the straps of our sandals, we should be aware that following Jesus through the eye of the needle is probably going to cost us, financially or otherwise, everything we have.

> *When the disciples heard this they were astonished. "Who can be saved, then?" they said. Jesus gazed at them. "For you" he told them "this is impossible; for God everything is possible."*
> (Matt. 19:25–26)

Notes

1. Michael Ventura, "In the Eye of the Millennium," *Family Therapy Networker* (November–December 1999): 27–35.

3

Spirituality for a Global Age

Rembert G. Weakland, OSB

The challenge that our religious culture faces today is the urgent need to develop a spirituality of wholeness that I will call a relational spirituality. Before explaining what is meant by that phrase, some preliminary remarks are necessary.

First of all, we are living through an important moment in history when more and more people are looking for a valid spirituality for their lives. Sister Joan Chittister, recognizing that fact, has been in the forefront of indicating paths that have to be taken, most of these directions coming out of her knowledge of the Benedictine spiritual tradition and her sensitivity to the modern scene, especially with regard to the role of women in church and society. The desire for a deeper spirituality is not the same as having the knowledge of how to acquire one. Yet, like Benedict's description of the novice, what is important is the search for God. Without that desire, no spiritual journey will be undertaken. At this moment of history we can be thankful for the presence of this strong desire among so many in our culture, but we must also ask what are the challenges that it poses to all of us and what resources and wisdom do we have to draw on.

Secondly, there are several spiritualities in our culture that are thriving, but not all of them are to be recommended equally. Sometimes we hear spirituality talked of as if it were nothing but another means of therapy, a way of obtaining calm in the midst of stress and strain. Although a true spirituality can lead to inner peace and thus is therapeutic in the best sense of the word, that aim is not sufficient in itself. At times, through one's spirituality, one can find an oasis, an inner peace when all around is out of order. But often such spiritualities fail when they are most needed because they do not give to the practitioner a higher motivation, a way of seeing even the difficulties of life in some perspective. They do not help, the old masters of the spiritual life would say, to sustain us during the dark nights of the soul. That is because they do not give God a chance. Often they are not realistic but seek to preserve us from the reality of the world we must live in.

Thirdly, our American culture so often can lead to Pelagianism, a tendency to think that we, on our own, can arrive at some deeper stage of spirituality. We Americans grow up with the idea that we can do anything we want if only we strive hard enough. Relying on self is taught to us early on. In the spiritual life that can lead to disaster. It cuts God out of the plan. If our culture is Pelagian, our spirituality will tend also to be tainted by that kind of total self-reliance to the exclusion of God and others. Self-reliance is confused here with a kind of superhuman stance that does not want to recognize the need for others. Or we think that to become holy all we have to do is follow a given program minutely, that we can treat the spiritual life just like a course in weightlifting or gymnastics. We fail to recognize that each person is different, that there is no one-size-fits-all spiritual guide.

Fourthly, we sometimes see a spirituality around us that guarantees that we can go beyond ourselves in some kind of miraculous way. It is the opposite of the third danger just cited. Here we see people thinking that it is God who lifts them to make the jump shot that is beyond their normal capabilities. God will carry them first over the line in the race. God works overtime to make the practitioner of this spirituality superhuman. When one fails, however, it is never God's fault but always our own. When we win, God always gets the first credit. God, in this spirituality, becomes the *deus ex machina* to bring the believer, the practitioner, to a higher level of human competency. The practitioner becomes God's favorite in the competitive world we live in. We see this kind of spirituality dominant in the sports world. It is the prime component of muscular Christianity.

Finally, there is a tendency in some modern spiritualities to separate body and soul, to deal only with the latter, and to see the former as unimportant. Here, spirit is identified with human spirit and not the Holy Spirit. This is a strange phenomenon, since it comes at the same moment when the mainline Christian churches are rediscovering the importance of the body in all genuine spirituality. One is amazed, however, at how many people are in search of out-of-body experiences as the ones to be sought in any spiritual development. In this spirituality it is easy to believe in transmigration of souls, since the soul is separated from the body. Personal identity is sought in the soul, not in the whole person. Sometimes this spirituality can be evasive, wanting, that is, to evade this world and prematurely to live in an eschatological world that has not yet arrived.

Another aspect of this kind of spirituality is that it constantly seeks visions and extraordinary phenomena. What the gospel demands in terms of spirituality becomes confused with signs and the extraordinary. When I was a student in Rome after World War II, many of my fellow students were running to Loreto to see Padre Pio. My response to their invitation to come along was always, "I have to live with saints day after day and it isn't easy. Why travel miles to see another?"

The great danger in all these spiritualities that flood the market today is that they tend to reinforce the individualism so rampant in our culture. All these spiritualities are "me" oriented. They ultimately force people to close in on themselves and they augment their isolation. They do not lead to wholeness but deformity. Most of them, in addition, leave no room for creativity and spontaneity. When they seem to cease to serve the purpose of the personal ego, when they begin to demand discipline and sacrifice, they are easily abandoned and a newer, easier, more satisfying project is taken up in the endless quest for easy or cheap holiness.

By contrast, what kind of spirituality is needed for our times? One that is relational. A spirituality that does not include a clear relationship to God, to others, to the universe around us, will ultimately not be real or helpful. On the contrary, any other kind will ultimately fail to provide what is most needed in our times.

Our culture is now global. To seek a spirituality that does not take this globalization into account will lack the ingredients needed to live a full and wholesome life. Sister Joan Chittister, by her writings and her levels of interest, can show us the way in this regard. Like a true religious, she sees her charism, not only as local, but also containing the germ of the global. Before many of us had thought of it, she was living in that global world, never failing to challenge herself and us to have a higher vision. Religious life should have that view of the world and of the church. Actualized locally, it still has a universal quality about it. There is no room for provincialism in today's world, and any sign of an exclusively inward-looking search for identity with no relationship to the rest of the world is simply empty and useless. Because our culture today is global, our spirituality must be global.

Such a global spirituality presupposes that God not only exists, but that God is present and operative in the whole world, not just in me and my little universe. One begins by putting no limits on the action of the Holy Spirit. The Spirit that is operative in me and that is forming me is the same Spirit that created the world. It is the same

Spirit that animated Jesus Christ, the one he bequeathed to his church, that is out ahead of us creating God's kingdom among us. A global spirituality is not possible without an intuition of the global action of the Spirit. But since that Spirit is a Spirit of love, one has to become a part of a spirituality that involves love on a global plane.

Such a spirituality is relational in that it first of all relates the person to God and to God's creative Spirit of love. God's role comes first. It cannot be Pelagianistic, or self-centered. God is always the prime actor. One is just as involved in discerning the action of the Spirit in oneself and in the world as in doing things. One lives in the marvel of God's love and the manifestations of that love all over the world. God is never left out, but God is not used for our personal gains and purposes.

A relational spirituality also brings us into contact with others. The closer we draw to Jesus Christ and the Spirit that animated him, the closer we draw to all other human beings. The greatest mystics in the Christian tradition knew that being close to Jesus Christ meant being close to others. We cannot in these end times separate Christ from all his hangers-on. Such a spirituality is relational in that we are drawn to others, not by our needs or our wants, but by the mere fact of our oneness with Christ in the Spirit. We live in a communion of saints and also in a communion of sinners. Liturgy, worship, the proclamation of the Bible — all of these traditional means of spirituality draw us toward others. That is why they must be recouped in our day. They must challenge us and draw us out of ourselves into service of others. Such a spirituality that is relational to Christ is also relational to others. This holds true especially toward the least fortunate, toward the poor. A spirituality that does not help one to identify with the poor and the needy on this globe is not worth its salt. We find ourselves in finding Christ in others. The rest is deception.

A global, relational spirituality is the most urgent spiritual need of our times. The qualities necessary for such a global spirituality I recognized some thirty years ago in Sister Joan Chittister when I asked her to be a member of the International Commission for Benedictine Sisters. It was a wise choice, as her later travels, interests, and writings showed. Through the years she has deepened her Benedictine roots, enlarged her local perspectives, engaged the globe and its needs, and learned how to articulate the results in a clear and cogent voice. In doing so she has challenged us all in the way the religious and prophetic charism should.

The charism of every religious congregation, it should be clear, is not for the members themselves but for the whole church. It is the church that, first of all, needs to be shaken out of its complacency, cajoled out of its fears of the present and anxieties for the future. A Catholic church should not fear the globalization that is characteristic of our age, but be eager for the challenge to evolve the spirituality that will make engaging that world exciting and fruitful. Sister Joan Chittister knew that years ago. We are all now slowly catching up with her.

4

Filtered by the Grapes

Janet Martin Soskice

How nice to be asked to write something for Joan Chittister. And I have been given a question to address: What is the most important spiritual question of our time? This question, this question about a question, is surrounded by silence. Am I the only one being asked to address this theme or have many, perhaps all, of the contributors been asked to diagnose our spiritual present and future? If so, would a consensus emerge? I can think of many possible answers — a spirituality for the poor, for women, one that addresses the environment (better known as creation). Why, then, do I find myself shying away from these answers?

If pressed, I would have an answer. I would say, "Grapes — good grapes. How to nurture good grapes?" That is the most important spiritual question of our time.

A lesson to be learned from Joan, and from the other followers of God whom the New Testament is pleased to call saints, is that God wants originals. How do we know? Because those are the only kind of people God makes. The God of the Bible does not have a generic love for persons, dogs, or high mountains — God loves everything *in particular*.

And as for the grapes? There are some things all grapevines need — soil, sun, water, length of days — but this says little. A vintner will tell you that every particular grape variety is specific in taste and tang. Furthermore, every actual vine grows on some particular soil, at some particular height, facing some particular direction, at some particular altitude and latitude. And every year in which this vine bears fruit has its own pattern of rain, or sun, or blight. Even before the distinctive choices by the vintner in the winemaking process, the juice of these vines itself is, every year, every month, distinct.

My husband and I had dinner with a farmer in Italy. He had a small holding with a few cattle, rabbits, corn, and grapevines from which he made his own wine. "Drink," he said, "drink." (We were on our honeymoon.) "You will not get a hangover, for this wine is absolutely pure!" Wine, he explained, is the purest form of water, because it has been filtered by the grape.

This, I thought, was a good way to consider my new husband's occupation as a painter. "Painting is the purest form of visibility, because it has been filtered by the painter." Paintings do not replace the beauty of the world around us, of course, any more than wine replaces water, but they teach us to appreciate what is there and what is everyday — so common as to be overlooked — the beauty of an apple or the joy of a glass of cold, clear water. We see these things incandescently in the beauty of the Creator.

And is this not what a theologian does, or for that matter, anyone who prays? In our own particular soil and space we take in the warmth of Scripture, and nourishment from tradition and community, and mix these with the specific joys and brickbats that life throws at us. (The best wines may not come from broad, sunny slopes but from vines that grow in torturous and difficult positions.) The point is not that the products of one grape are the best, but that all are different. It is the task of the vinekeeper to savor and nurture these grapes, to see how the tart acidity of the one juice may be complemented by the fresh, raspberry flavor of another. In some seasons a particular vine may bear little fruit, or bad.

This grape harvest is the lives of the saints who make up on earth the body of Christ — lives of some who have ruled kingdoms and of others who have remained quietly at home tending an aged parent or a troubled child; lives of great athletes and of those for whom every movement presents a painful challenge, including some great athletes who later in life grow to find every movement difficult. All these moments make up the specificity and the bouquet of the final wine.

And so, "Grapes — good grapes." The most important spiritual question of our time is how to love in one another the glorious diversity with which our Maker has made us, not seeking one template for perfection but loving the difference. In the end, the great Vinekeeper will — in ways we have never anticipated — bring together all these particular tastes and tangs to make the wine of the kingdom of heaven.

5

The Need for Spiritual Moorings

Martin E. Marty

The best way for me to frame an answer to "What is the most important spiritual question of our time?" is to relate it to two incidents. I am going to argue that the question and the response to it has two aspects.

First, let me contrast "spiritual" to "material," which is the ancient way of dividing the subject. I have to say in passing that this will not be a diatribe against the material. As a Christian I rejoice in the materiality of this faith. An Anglican divine with a sense of humor and a pithy mode of expression condensed it well: "Christianity is *very* material. You can't even get or keep it going without a loaf of bread, a bottle of wine, and a river." Attach an "ism" to material, however, and everything looks different.

Yawn. One more complaint about materialism? Let me refine it a bit more and say that a particular version of concern with the material is what is distracting majorities in our cultures and societies from drawing on spiritual resources that have depth.

So here is the first incident. In my last year of teaching I made the rounds of the alumni circuit, sharing the stage on several occasions with an international economist of note. He would begin by stepping forward with good news and bad news.

The "good news," he trumpeted brightly, was that the market had won. It had simply won. Communist societies had imploded, and even surviving nominal communist nations, such as China, had gone capitalist in their economy. Radical socialisms were also lifeless. Collectivism was out. The market had won. That was good news to a University of Chicago economist, where pro-market talk wins Nobel prizes.

My colleague, however, was not a shallow public relations agent for the market. He moved quickly and with change of demeanor to the "bad news." The bad news is that we — the cultures of the West and more than these — have not the faintest idea with what personal and social philosophies we will greet the change.

Some will argue that capitalism will be the "ism" that will serve to gather up all the strands of free-market, free-enterprise talk. I have read all the Christian apologies for capitalism, and am not going to go on record as claiming that there is nothing to be said for versions of it. But at root there is an anthropology, an understanding of human nature and existence, that works itself out in ways that seem patently contradictory to the gospel.

In my book there is no "ism" that will be simply congruent with the Christian message, including Christianism, any sort of systematic way of connecting the gospel promises and commands with forms of government or economic life. But I believe that there can be, there are, elements of philosophies, outlooks, and ways of life that can help us interpret, judge, and direct the emergent global market economy.

The Benedictine way of life offers some clues. So do the career and writings of a Benedictine named Sister Joan Chittister. These ways and themes can take their place as thoughtful Christians and thoughtful Everybody Elses who do not want to be captivated and enthralled by the market triumph fashion responses.

Who would deny the fact that four-fifths of the American people are sharing in the most sustained, comfortable, and even luxurious way of life this nation or, no doubt, any nation has known? The same fact has helped the four-fifths forget about the others, those who make up the rural and urban underclass — can we find a better word? — that will be the legacy of these highest times.

The toll the triumphant market takes on marriage and family, church and associational life, nerves and personalities gets documented daily. Compulsive competition at work and obsessive pursuits of leisure, with the instruments of cyberspace and high technology at hand to interfere anywhere, anytime, are signals of the problem.

Through it all I have kept perspective on what is going on by reference to Psalm 106. To paraphrase it, the people of God had asked for everything: freedom, new land, home, prosperity. God gave them what they wanted. But then, in the King James Version, God "sent leanness into their souls." In the Jerusalem Bible, God "struck them with a deep wasting sickness." How to address and heal — that is the most important spiritual question of our time.

And now, part two: how to go about addressing it? Here I want to sneak in the other dimension of a two-phased issue. If at first we played with the material/spiritual dialectic, now the focus falls on what our culture has come to call "spirituality" in its yin and yang relation to "community," as in church.

Spirituality used to come packaged with communal attachments.

Look up the word in the *Reader's Guide to Periodical Literature* any time before the 1970s and you will find adjectives such as "Medieval," "Jewish," "Catholic," and the like coloring it. In the 1970s we began to read of "spiritual spirituality," the seeking-searching-striving-journeying pattern one finds in the megabookstore sections that used to be marked "religion," or sees and hears about among upper-middle-class Americans who "hate" organized religion, are not members of "the institutional church," are not sure they are religious, but who assure everyone else that they are *very* spiritual.

Now, grump, get off this polemic! You cannot hang out with Benedictines without being drawn into a profound spiritual sphere; here is the *ora* that goes with the *labora* of Benedictine life. Prayer, meditation, liturgy, devotional reading, the mystical quest — all enhancements to life near God, life in God. What has gone wrong has been the sundering of this spiritual affect and aspiration from community, tradition, texts, shared experience.

And when that severing occurs, spirituality can become one more commodity that fits in well with "having it all" and "getting the wasting sickness." One can prefer those in the spiritual search over the old mid-twentieth-century model of "secular man" — yes, man — and still see that such a search can lead not to, but away from, action, from seeing and addressing human need and working for justice or spreading mercy.

When one seeks an outlook with which to address the new materialism and a deeper way to pursue spirituality, it helps to be in community, be it a congregation, a parish, a cell, a movement, a cause, or whatever. There participants can be judged by texts that have weathered time and survived in many cultures. There we "bear one another's burdens and so fulfill the law of Christ." In such community we can be admonished and cheered, cajoled and congratulated.

Robert Wuthnow had made a helpful distinction between what he calls "dwelling spirituality" and "seeker spirituality." He suggests we pursue "practical spirituality," which includes aspects of both. Dwelling spirituality means having an abode, a place to go and to be, whether this be in something as reaching as "the Church Catholic" or a reading group that has continuity. It does not "make up spirituality as it goes along," but pays respect to the inherited intuitive wisdom of suffering, struggling people in various cultures. It does not take religion "a la carte," in a pick-and-choose mold, but it also is not exclusive, enclave building. One can go very deep in a faith tradition and there meet "the other" with more openness and freedom than might the spiritual dabbler.

My own way of speaking about this is to see spirituality "moored" or "unmoored." We are all on the high seas much of the time — occasionally becalmed, often in storm, sometimes in fog. But those with moorings know where to go to get new bearings and supplies. The unmoored cast about without compass, now and then finding a harbor, a lighthouse, a port in the storm, before pushing on to who knows where.

Oh, I promised a second incident to color these theses. I was speaking to about two hundred hospital chaplains — pastors and priests — and lay ministers who call on the hospitalized and those who are ill in other venues. Somewhere along the way someone asked what I had against "spirituality" as such in this area, and it came to mind that "Spirituality does not make hospice calls." That is not a slam at the many isolated people who shun congregational and associational life but are ethical, generous, given to justice and mercy alike. But they are not organized for or impelled to carry on sustained work.

It is often said that today the path to spirituality is the path of action. Not compulsive action, as in the material quest that commodifies everything and makes consumerists of us all. But action that recognizes the call of the Spirit in the neighbor in need. That is not content with the way the world is momentarily put together. That is the expression of people who are not content with saying that the market has won, and that's good news and bad news. Instead, it proclaims and is graced by the Really Good News that will outlast current economic and political structures and bring healing in the face of "wasting disease" in the culture and in the soul.

6

The Saber-Toothed Tiger

Brother Thomas Bezanson

With souls we are born;
Spirit we must acquire.
— ABRAHAM HESCHEL

In his famous treatise *The Phenomenon of Man,* Teilhard de Chardin wrote of hyperspecialization that occurred along the curve of evolution — specialization paralyzes, hyperspecialization kills. For example, the saber-toothed tiger by ultraspecialization of tooth and claw created a morphological prison for its species. The efficiency of what it had developed and developed into left no room for adaptation to the compression of change in the process of a becoming world. It had become its own world, not a part of the world.

It does not take a paleontologist, however, to make an analogy with our own species, *Homo sapiens,* so patently creating the means of its own destruction, not from within itself, but because it has forgotten that it has a self within.

We are created in the image of God with a goal of mirroring that image in our world. The means of fulfilling that goal is the radical gift of freedom and, because of the very nature of the gift of freedom, *Homo sapiens* can choose, paradoxically, to be unfree. And again, because the first extensions of the power of freedom are creativity and love, the inversion of freedom can roll back upon itself in uncreative, unloving acts of destruction and hate. Creativity and love are the yardsticks of freedom, and freedom through acts of creativity and love are the dynamism of our authentic becoming.

In our era, to all but the most anesthetized among us, *Homo sapiens* is obviously running with its gift of freedom in reverse, running back upon itself in acts of destruction.

Through so many cold-war years, the world community lived with the fear that somewhere, someone would push that red button of nuclear destruction. While the possibility of nuclear annihilation is far from eliminated in our world, at least the height of that fear has been lowered.

But in today's world, except for a special vision here and there, we are blind to the red buttons of slow destruction that are pushed everywhere, everyday, by all of us in some measure. We may not all be guilty, but we are all responsible.

Every year we scatter millions of tons of toxic waste into the center of life. Every year we destroy thousands of species, and not just individual plants and animals, but their entire heritage of DNA. We are not killing elephants; we are killing Elephant. When those unique cosmic substances are gone, they are gone forever.

How abundant is water on this Eden planet. How rare it is in the rest of the known universe. We do not just *have* water; largely, we ourselves *are* water. Yet, we are poisoning whole aquifers and polluting the oceans, presuming upon a nonexistent technology to fix everything. Our science culture has produced a state of mind that is largely a delusion, a muddle that has become a mess.

The air, the water, the soil — when we poison these things, upon which our very existence depends, we are destroying ourselves. It is difficult to wrap our minds around the reality of species destruction, much less grasp the finality of DNA extinction, and we seem totally chloroformed to the possibility that in the end, it could be our own. We are always prepared for the worst but never for the inconceivable.

Yet, the inner sense of our species remains vital and knows that our present activities do not speak of who we are in our very seed. It all hinges on forgetting or remembering that *Homo sapiens* has an interior reality, that is, the seed of spiritual becoming, and an exterior revelation of how to live and how not to live to bring it to flower in ourselves and in our world. Perhaps we will soon awaken to see that a race we once argued was the end point of evolution, the center of the cosmos, is in fact only the beginning of something new, that, in a word, *Homo sapiens* is not the *Homo humanis* we are called to be.

To be sure, lest we forget entirely, here and there, now and then, great persons have blipped out of the becoming curve as witness to human possibility — the prophets of Israel, Jesus of Nazareth, Buddha, Mohammed, Gandhi, Mother Teresa, Martin Luther King Jr. — and they still do, all around us, in all the known and anonymous men and women of spiritual wholeness. They sustain the infolding and unfolding of human becoming. What they model is there for us also to choose through acts of creativity and love.

One of the enduring signs of the universal human seed within us is an irrepressible appetite for the things of a spiritual life, that is, what is good, what is true, what is beautiful, and ultimately for what unites and does not divide. It is an ancient illumination of what to live for and what not to live for. In our era the march toward hyperindividualization is a march in the opposite direction of what the human seed hungers for: unity with others, synthesis with all that is.

It is the fatal flaw in our science culture that regards the whole and healthy to be the one who is capable of standing alone. It is a radical confusion between individual and person. Hyperindividualization is an analog of Teilhard's "specialization paralyzes, hyperspecialization kills." The possibility of human transformation is at a conspicuous low in this kind of culture. Becoming "number one" is no substitute for becoming One.

What is missing? We focus on the intelligence of our species and define ourselves by our rationality. But it is not intelligence that is missing. It is *reflective consciousness,* a power beyond intellect without which we are just another, more rational animal. All animals are conscious; that is, they know. But it is only the human animal that knows that it knows, and that is an altogether other power.

We reflect, bend back, infold on what we know, who we are, where we are going. We question. Reflective consciousness is an *actus humanus,* not merely an *actus hominis.* It is an act of a spiritual being, not merely of a biological being.

Reflective consciousness is a far different kind of rolling back upon oneself than rolling back upon oneself in the biological order. In that order we are as fixed in our being and becoming as all the other animals. But in the order of reflective consciousness we are outside the vectors of natural selection. We can act, we can choose, based on what we know we know.

The unfolding of the whole universe rests on the principle *action follows being.* As a being is, so does it act. Everything from the micro to the macro performs faithfully to the music of its being. The principle applies to every living creature except one — us.

In us, on the level of human becoming, that principle is reversed: *being follows action.* It is reversed in us because of our freedom. Freedom is our exemption from the determinacy of the universal principle that action follows being. It is reversed because of our reflective consciousness — the power to commission our inner being, our person. It moves us into a state of autoevolution. With every animal in creation we share many things, including intelligence, but not this one thing: the consciousness that I am I and no other.

If, then, we hunger for a human kingdom of the good, the true, the beautiful, for an Eden of at-one-ment, it will not happen unless we choose those activities of becoming that create the human being itself. The well-worn aphorism of Socrates, "Know thyself," would have done the Western soul a radical good if the "wisest of all" had paused, reflected, and said instead, "Create thyself." Then would that originator of our science culture have set our feet on a more humanizing path than the labyrinths of knowledge and the conceits of the IQ.

For the first time in the course of Earth's becoming, the dynamism of self-evolution is rooted in a being with the freedom to choose its own becoming, the reflective consciousness to know it, and the creative intelligence to shape it. We are at the cosmic crossroads of choosing a spiritual evolution — a critical crossroads, for unless our being becomes a spiritual being, we won't be at all. Alas, there is a famine in the land, and the will to transformation hungers unheard.

That statement in the Christian Scriptures which reads, "Many are called but few are chosen," would serve us better rewritten, "All are called but few are choosing."

Some doors open only from inside. The door to a true humanity is one of them.

7

Who Do You, God, Say That We Are?

Diana L. Hayes

Where are we going? Why do we act in the ways that we do? Where will it all end? Is there a purpose, a reason for our existence, or is all life simply happenstance? Despite the negative prophecies by scientists of the nineteenth and twentieth centuries, religion persists and human beings still ask questions that science has been unable to answer about their own existence and the world around them. In the last century most of the questions have dealt with the issue of "who God is for us" as human beings. How do we see God and God's actions in our lives? Is God still actively engaged in human history or has God retreated to the heavens, observing with a cold and austere eye our fumbling attempts at becoming like gods ourselves?

We have been so busy asking who God is for us that we have forgotten that we were made for God, not God for us. God cannot be captured in a box, in a church, mosque, temple, or synagogue, nor in a piece of music, a prayer, rite, or ritual. God is in all of these and so much more. We cannot control God's being by defining or describing it any more than God seeks to control ours. But in our haste to get ahead we have lost sight of the fullness of our freedom, boxing ourselves into narrow concepts and understandings of both God and humanity. We think we have captured God's essence, as well as our own, only to discover in time that we have captured nothing but ourselves.

Is this the question for the next century, that asked by Jesus of Peter: "Who do you say that I am?" I would argue that the question has changed. Unlike the people of the first century or even of the eighteenth, we are no longer in touch with ourselves, with our humanity, with our creatureliness as beings created by a loving God. We have, for the most part, lost contact with our inner selves, which have been psychoanalyzed into a quivering mass of naked psychoses.

To be a spirit-filled person, one with an intimate relationship with an all-powerful, all-loving Being beyond human finitude, has come to be seen as a fault or failure, something to be scorned and rejected, analyzed, examined, and eradicated as a weakness. The freedom and beauty of a spiritual life, closely connected with and inseparable from one's everyday life, has been twisted and turned into a neatly defined package of teachings, beliefs, and acts that must be adhered to at all costs. Anyone whose expression of the spirit does not conform to this neatly wrapped box is seen as heretical or psychically immature.

Faith in something or someone greater than oneself is suspect in today's business-oriented, individualistic world. It is seen as a harmful dependency. Yet peoples throughout the world, especially in the highly industrialized nations, find themselves at a loss, seeking after something or someone, or some meaning in their lives that they cannot even name. There is an emptiness within them that all of the busyness of their overscheduled and highly organized lives cannot seem to fill. That yearning is not being answered by our churches, our synagogues, or any of the other traditional forms of institutional religion. Perhaps this is so because these institutions have become so involved in naming and thereby controlling the Spirit that they no longer have it within their midst. Once the arbiters of social, cultural, moral, and even political mores, they are increasingly seen as enclaves of the elite or as moral policemen, sites of condemnation and judgment rather than of welcome and affirmation. The roles once seen as their preserve have been taken over by other, private and public organizations without any religious affiliation. They have lost that which they sought and claimed to own and have become "whitened sepulchers" devoid of life, of knowledge, of hope, of the spirit.

Many people have turned to other sources, religious and otherwise, seeking to satisfy their hunger for meaning. All the while, they seem unable to comprehend that the answer lies within themselves and those around them. For the answer to their eternal questions of self and belonging, the answer to the paramount question for this age, "Who am I and why?" can only be God in God's self and as God is reflected in the faces of all of our fellow human beings. For we have truly lost our way in the world. We have turned against each other, refusing to acknowledge the Other's humanity and godliness because today the Other is no longer just like us, if ever she or he was. The Other has a different skin color, speaks a different language, and worships in a different style or manner, albeit the same God. And this point is critical. We worship the same God, however that God may be named, but allow human difference to separate and alienate us rather than to draw us together. Yet, how can we seek out God while ignoring God's presence in our very midst?

Who, God, do you say that we are? If only we had the courage to ask this question of our Creator God and, more importantly, were able really to be open to God's answer, our lives and our world would surely be transformed. Instead, we waste our time chasing down blind alleys, worshiping false gods of wealth and possessions, searching in strange places, listening to the voices of false prophets who promise what they cannot provide while ignoring the truth that stares us in the face. The truth is that we are one people, breathed into life by a loving God who gave us the freedom to live, prosper, multiply, and be the stewards of all of God's creation.

Who am I? What is the purpose of my being here? Is not the answer to this deeply existential question simply, God? Who am I? I am a child of God, whether black, brown, yellow, red, or white, because race does not exist in God. Nor do other divisions exist in God, not those of Muslim, Jew, Christian, Hindu, or other, because God is God for all of humanity however God is named. No matter if one is male or female, rich or poor, young or old, we are all created in God's own image and likeness, a creation that God declared to be good without caveats. Why am I here on this earth at this time and place? To help bring about God's *kin-dom* by recognizing and, more importantly, by affirming my co-createdness with all of humanity and thus the presence of God in all with whom I come into contact. I am called, as all are called, to contribute to the rebuilding of community, a community in which all are welcome, receiving according to their needs and offering according to their abilities.

Those who are the least among us already know the answer to this most critical spiritual question for our time: "Who do you, God, say that I, humanity, am?" This is not because their lives are so simple and childlike that spirituality naturally flourishes in their midst, but because they, like Job, have been tested and survived. Their everyday lives are such a constant struggle simply to survive in the face of genocide, massacre, war, rape, poverty, and life-threatening illnesses that they are drawn ever closer to God, who is the answer to all of our longings, all of our hungers, all of our yearnings.

"Our hearts are restless until they rest in thee, O Lord." Surely, St. Augustine spoke the truth. For he too knew that lust and greed could consume one's very existence, filling one's life with supposedly all that one could wish for but somehow still leaving an echoing, gnawing emptiness within the core of one's being. This emptiness is our hunger for God, for someone or something greater than ourselves, who transcends our everyday world and carries us beyond that world, enabling us to have hope.

Is it not time for us to learn from the example of those who have suffered the most and yet have a rich, nurturing life of the spirit that enables them to persevere in their daily struggle? For God is present and appears to us in the faces of those least like us, those from whom we turn away in anger, in disgust, in shame. We must learn from them. We must learn to listen to them, to work with them, to help to alleviate their suffering often caused by our greed and insensitivity. At the same time, we must try to understand who they are in themselves, rather than perceive them as objects of our charity or pity. We must also learn how, in the midst of their pain and anguish, they are still able to continue to walk and talk with God.

Difference is not dangerous; it is of God. Difference has been divinely sanctioned in the act of creation. It is our responsibility, as sharers in that creation, to turn away from divisiveness and move toward community. For we are all our brothers' and sisters' keepers. God has placed upon all of us the responsibility of following in God's own footsteps, of loving all people as God loves us, of seeking their greater good rather than our own individual success. We can only do this by letting go of the "isms" that continue to plague humanity — negativisms based on race, ethnicity, gender, class, sexual orientation, and religious creed. We must begin to remove the blinders we have placed on ourselves that restrict our vision, blinding us to the light of God shining through the face of all God's people. We must come together as one, seeking to build a community of the faithful that rejects a narrow, dualistic, biased perception of life.

"Who do you, God, say that we are?" We are your children, lost and wandering in a confusing and confused world, but never abandoned, never forsaken, never alone. We are your chosen ones, given knowledge of life and death, and the ability through your grace to use that knowledge to choose life in all of its diversity and to transform this world into your reign. This is our challenge for the coming century and perhaps for the new millennium. May we continue to be blessed with the wisdom and love of God in order to reclaim our full life in the Spirit and be transformed.

8

God and Rice Bowls in a New Age

Christine Vladimiroff, OSB

When I was a child, I was told to eat everything on my plate because children were hungry in China. I even saved my pennies in mite boxes during Lent to fill their rice bowls. Along with the other children I "bought" pagan babies and felt relieved that they were safe and baptized because of our sacrifices. Through the faith of my parents and the zeal of my Catholic education I was a child missionary and a three-and-a-half-foot-tall social activist in the primary grades.

Reflecting on that past, I wonder how I could have had such a vivid picture of what faith looked like in action. Growing up in an era before television, I saw no pictures of emaciated refugees walking toward humanitarian food aid stations. I could not see with my own eyes the babies with swollen stomachs or the despair in the faces of parents watching their children die. The urgency to act out of faith was created in me by listening to words. They were words spoken to me by believing and caring parents whose parenthood embraced all children. They were words spoken in deep faith by dedicated teachers, nuns, who saw the salvation of the world as their personal responsibility. That was remarkable in a time when the term "global village" did not exist.

It was so clear to me at a young age that faith demanded action. It was so clear to me that my life was linked to others who shared the globe with me. Yet, we did not have the concept of a social ecosystem, but just faith that we were part of a communion of saints. I marvel at how real those truths were for me. I am grateful to those who mentored me in my faith, for I have built my adult life on those foundational understandings. The spirituality I received taught me to embrace the world.

In this millennium, technology makes global linkages possible in real time. Pictures of disasters in Africa and the voices of victims are seen and heard in our living rooms simultaneously with the events unfolding. But, without high-tech, I can walk down the street in any major city in the United States and see the hungry and the homeless. I can reach out and touch them and look into their eyes as I toss my coin in their direction. How do I respond out of faith in this new time? What spirituality must I have to be authentic in my response to new circumstances?

In our day a person is more apt to be flooded with images and data and still cultivate the fine art of remaining untouched and aloof. We know how to be alone in an age of mobile phones, caller ID, and cyberconnections. We are highly protective of our space and what we let into our lives. Is "compassion fatigue" possible for people of faith?

In a global world, "Love your neighbor" has international consequences. What spirituality can lead us to live our faith with this new awareness? In what way can we pass on our faith to a new generation that will not only accept responsibility for the poor, but also for the very earth and air that sustain life on our planet? How can we capture the imagination of the young with the vision that the human family is one?

These are serious considerations, and if we do not have adequate answers, there are consequences for our world. We need to pass on a vibrant faith, and a spirituality that inserts a person into a very interdependent world. That spirituality must be a source of courage to risk new and creative expressions of compassion and care. It must be a mature spirituality that will use new structures and institutions to bring grace and goodness to the forgotten people and places on our planet. Wisdom is needed to fashion structures of inclusion as we shape the social, economic, and political realities of a new age.

Spirituality cannot be a screen for creating distance and detachment from life. Abraham Heschel tells us that a person immersed in the prophets' words is an individual exposed to a ceaseless shattering of indifference. It is remembering the prophetic call to seek justice that has the capacity to move a generation, not only to feed the hungry, but also to dismantle the structures of greed that keep children malnourished. The prophetic word is a conflictive word. It will put us at odds with whatever is not of the reign of God in this new century. Those of us who have grown in faith must model the way and bring the vision to the young.

A "feel good" spirituality will not be adequate to the challenge. Nor will a spirituality that defines flight from, rather than engagement with, the world as holy. The methods of prayer are unimportant unless they lead to a life lived in the presence of God. The exotic is not to be confused with what is effective in the spiritual life.

For the church's legacy of faith in action to be passed on requires a call to conversion for the institutional church. It was the experience of community that carried the words and the example of persons living their faith to my mind and heart as a child. It was the lived commitment that I saw and a daily fidelity that taught me that gospel living was about passion and not about regulations. Church life today must convey to the young and old that holiness is an ardent embrace of life in this time and place. Community supports the conviction that slowly grows in each of us that our life has a purpose and that we can make a difference.

Today, I see a sense of community in groups working for change in the church and in society. It is faith in action at gatherings of a jubilee people calling for international debt cancellation — perhaps this is the modern equivalent of my Lenten mite box to fill the rice bowls of the Chinese children. It is the life of an Oscar Romero, which tells me that the conflictive word of a prophet can bring death to those who utter it but life to those who live on after them. Life, after all, Jesus taught us, is to be given away for the sake of others.

Humans seek community and a way to commit the force of their being to something greater than themselves. Authentic spirituality will give the believer both the experience of belonging and the opportunity for giving life meaning. It will also leave a legacy for those who follow.

The history of spirituality is rich with trends and patterns. Each age defined the particular ways men and women gave value and direction to their lives as followers of Jesus. The spirituality of an age marks both our corporate lives as church and our individual lives as believers. The twentieth century was remarkable in the diversity of expressions of spirituality. They grew as a response to the events of the times. At times they coexisted with and gave new insights to our way of living out belief. An example would be the revival and renewal of monastic life and its effect on the spirituality of the layperson after World War II. This was in part a response to the horror observed in war and the depth of personal conversion it occasioned. Leaders emerged in persons such as Thomas Merton in the Catholic community and Roger Schultz of Taizé in the ecumenical community. Their writings and lived examples of community and commitment caught the spirit of the God-seekers.

A new shift came later with the Second Vatican Council, which brought the beginnings of a transformational process yet to gather full power in the church. The biblical movement and new scholarship gave us identity as a people of God. We reclaimed the ancient spirituality of service and ministry as an authentic expression of who we found ourselves to be in God's eyes. The liturgical renewal movement presented a dynamic spirituality and sense of sacramental life in a world full of God's presence. There was openness to the Other in ecumenical efforts beyond polite collaboration, which influenced our thinking about salvation and theology. The Latin American church on our borders taught us a liberation theology that gave us a new spirituality, a new way to look at the poor and be evangelized by them. This same liberation theology was the impetus to help us deal with the racism and sexism found in society and the church. We were influenced in how to live our Christian faith in the world that was ours at that moment. Liberation spirituality holds an understanding of faith that stretches our soul to respond to what diminishes us as a people and what is disruptive of right relationships.

Thus, with the accelerated pace of change we cannot afford to have a spirituality that is frozen in the past. We must search for an animating spirituality and articulate clearly that faith is linked to life in this new century. We do not have the certitudes of the past. We have new questions. The structures and institutions change and we must search beyond them to find personal value and significance in our faith life. We were made for God. The human spirit is lured by holiness. Genuine prayer produces an uneasy discontent with the status quo. Our musing leads us deeper on an interior journey. The emergent passion from our God-seeking expresses itself in our living life intentionally, deliberately. With new energy we challenge conventional wisdom. Our acts take us to the edge of what is safe personally, socially, and politically. An authentic spirituality radically redefines the way we live in the world. No relationship is untouched by our quest to be holy.

Will this new spirituality be open and creative enough to address a life that might have us traveling and living on other planets? What in our spiritual development will give meaning to additional years in the human life span made possible by medicine and technology? Will we shape a spirituality that can help us make wise decisions with our new knowledge and the power we possess from biomedical advances? Will our acknowledgement of the presence of God in our lives help us avoid ecological catastrophes and the famine and epidemics they bring? How will we explain the presence of poverty among such abundance and possibilities? How do we stop the killing — capital punishment, ethnic cleansing, and war?

I am no longer that little girl in grade school. I am an adult struggling with today's questions. I do not expect easy answers, but companions who will join me in the search to live a holy life here and now. Joan Chittister opens the definition and function of spirituality when she writes, "Spirituality is about developing the courage, the determination, to commit ourselves to living all the dimensions of life with awareness and strength, with depth and quality." To this I can only say, "Amen."

9

Rebirthing God in the New Millennium

Edwina Gateley

In the last few decades a growing disillusionment with institutionalized religion has made a major impact on the Western world. This disillusionment affects millions of people as they slowly, and even painfully and reluctantly, drift away from participation in ritual, liturgy, and faith community. They are not, however, carrying on their lives as if they had just shed extra and unnecessary luggage; on the contrary, the loss experienced by vast numbers of people leaves a deep vacuum that has yet to be filled. This vacuum underlines, I believe, one of the most important spiritual questions of our time: Who and where is God, here and now, in the third millennium? The death of God forecast by theologians over the last forty years is now an experienced reality for increasing numbers of people in the Christian community.

The question of God cannot be asked in isolation, for it is central to our understanding of the world, humanity, and our relationship to each other and to all that exists. As such, the question impacts our self-understanding, and our self-understanding gives meaning, or not, to our raison d'être and our role in the universe.

Like it or not, we are shedding, inexorably and irretrievably, images and symbols of God that have defined our self-understanding for the past millennium. It has indeed taken us a long time to get to this dearth in which we now live. Our Hebrew ancestors in the Jewish tradition enjoyed a male warrior God, Yahweh, who led them from victory to victory and demanded in return sacrifice and obedience; Jesus tempered such a Deity with the compassionate face of a God who was Abba, Father, and who demanded mercy not sacrifice. The Christian church, which was founded on the Jesus experience, started as a charismatic healing and preaching community and eventually became the most powerful religious organization in the world. As such, it developed numerous rites, symbols, rules, canons, doctrines, and liturgies to express and contain the religious experience of its adherents. These structures and symbols helped nurture the worshiper's spirituality, which manifested itself in prayer and in an active life, the former more naturally done in church and the latter lived outside the church. (Although the faithful were encouraged to try to bring the two together — exactly how to do that has baffled most Christians for centuries.)

The Christian church, to which most of the Western world has adhered in the past, presents a Trinitarian Deity — Father, Son, and Spirit — all male and all external. The ecclesiastical structure is hierarchical and patriarchal which also reflects Western societal norms and classes. Such a God, such a religious institution, and indeed the spirituality that flows from it have never been as seriously questioned by so many as in our times. The last two decades have seen the relentless emptying of Christian churches, along with the exodus of thousands of their leaders. Our religious and, inevitably, our spiritual ground are, without doubt, shifting. And one indeed wonders whether it is well nigh time. The spirituality traditionally encouraged and nurtured by Western institutionalized religion is, for the most part, deeply personal and private. It flows from one's own piety, prayer life, and worship, and is directed toward the external Father God who watches over us. Certainly it is a most comforting and consoling spirituality. Its ultimate goal is a deepening personal relationship with God. And although Christians are constantly exhorted to love one another and do good works, these have not defined Christian spirituality as much as one's personal relationship with the divine "Other." The ultimate focus of our spirituality has been to gain access to a new and better life after this one — heaven. While waiting for heaven, however, the ground on which we stand has become increasingly unstable and unreliable.

After almost a millennium of a hierarchically conditioned "Other" and "otherworldly" spirituality, the human race and the earth on which we depend for survival have never been so threatened and so diminished. Violence is rampant. At any given time, over two dozen wars are being waged all over the globe. There is more poverty and disease today than ever in human history. In Africa alone over ten million children are left orphaned by the AIDS epidemic, which continues to rage throughout the continent and threatens its very destruction. The gap between the rich and poor in the developed countries continues to widen, and the international debt owed by the poor countries to the West cripples any attempt to improve the abysmal educational, health, and social conditions in those countries. Wars, ethnic cleansing, genocide, and terrorism all present horrific challenges to the developed world's claim to honor human rights. The pollution of international waters, the irreversible destruction of the world's forests, and increased toxic emissions into the air we breathe — these and other abuses of our planet leave us, on the cusp of the new millennium, a deeply shamed and far-from-spiritual people. Who and where is God for us?

It would seem quite clear that the King, Warrior, Judge, Father God whom we have so long been loving is not, in fact, about to save or rescue us in spite of numerous pleadings. This God, whom we have for generations relied on and depended on for vindication, shows no sign of punishing evildoers. On the contrary, human experience indicates that the evildoers seem, in general, to do rather well.

As we look in horror and despair at the pain and desperation of our world, once secure believers increasingly suspect, deep down, that God is not going to visit us with miracles, healing, and resurrection after all. At the same time, the spirituality we have long embraced and lived out seems to be increasingly irrelevant in the face of global chaos. In fact, it no longer even provides the solace and security it once did. There is instead an emptiness — a terrible vacuum that is being experienced by more and more once devout and unquestioning Christians. In the place of spiritual complacency and security comes a deep loneliness and, worse, a growing sense of loss and helplessness. The experience of many thinking Christians is that there is an absence of wisdom in how we live, how we relate to the rest of humanity, and how we deal with the world's problems. This realization cannot be separated from how we perceive ourselves in terms of being a spiritual people. If God is not going to save the world, who is? That question evokes a fearful sense of spiritual bankruptcy. Vast numbers of Christians are desperately trying to fend off the reality of a "dark night of the soul," which can no longer be denied as a widespread and destabilizing spiritual experience.

This can be a time of critical self-awareness, but a *new* kind of self-awareness — one that is related to the rest of the world — to all humanity, to all creatures, to our earth, and to our environment. Nudging into our psyches is a shift of consciousness that leaves us disturbingly but convincingly aware that we are all, somehow, connected, and that we are all, somehow, responsible for each other. This consciousness leaves many in a desert place — a place of not knowing. It is a wilderness place — a place of utter spiritual death. Who and where is God for us now? Where are our images? Who will comfort us? Do we need to discard our beloved images to create a space for this new consciousness to emerge? And what will this new consciousness look like?

The king is dead. The warrior gone. The judge silent. The father faded. All that upheld the traditional visions of God is vanishing from the reality of many people, and at this point in our religious history no one and no thing is adequately filling the vacancy left by the divine gap. As Thomas Berry once said, "It's all a question of story; we are in trouble just now because we are in between stories." Yet it is just such an experience of devastation and abandonment that traditionally contains the seeds of new life. Ezekiel was the spirit of Yahweh in the dry bones; Miriam took her timbrel and danced; Moses brought water from the rock and manna from heaven. The new has not yet come. But it must come. It must, because we stand, I believe, at the edge of the abyss. If we as a people do not call upon a truly empowering and transformative spirituality — a deeper wisdom that will impel us to action and to new life — then nations will continue to fight and to destroy, diseases will continue to wipe out generations, pollution will continue to poison our air and our oceans, and hunger will continue to kill the world's children. The challenge facing us at this time is to let go of the old images and the old belief system and to be open to a new and deeper consciousness — the stillpoint at the center of our being — that will lead us to relinquish our need for power, applause, security, and all the other things that have created our ego-centered lifestyles, and shift us toward a movement for deep inner peace and wisdom that can only connect us with each other.

The god that no longer leads us to victory, the god that no longer saves, must die. This means that in some way, we must die too. One of the most challenging spiritual questions facing us in this generation is, Dare we die? Dare we let go of a whole religious way of being that left most of us passively waiting to be saved and pursuing a personal, external God to the detriment of entering into a deep connection, a relationship with each other and the earth and taking the responsibility for its nurture and survival? Dare we let go of the security that such a God and such a religious conditioning gave us? And dare we come to recognize that we are indeed, as the mystic Meister Eckhart says, a seed of God, each called to be mother of God — that is, to actually give birth to the Holy ourselves.

In traditional Hebrew literature the Holy Spirit is Wisdom — Sophia, the feminine principle of the Godhead. She is depicted as artist, craftsperson, wife; she is the One who "waits at your gates" to be discovered and to begin the journey of new possibilities. Wisdom is not external. She dwells within, like Eckhart's God seed. Wisdom is available to all who call her. She is to be found by all who seek her with open hearts:

> Wisdom is bright, and does not grow dim,
> By those who love her she is readily seen
> And found by those who look for her....
> Watch for her early and you will have no trouble:
> You will find her sitting at your gates.
>
> (Wis. 6:12–14)

To encounter Sophia is to open oneself to the mystical experience. This is a profound and transforming awareness of the divine presence and potential *within* ourselves and our human condition. This awareness breaks open new possibilities and hope for our frightened world. If God is indeed at the core of the human condition — inseparable from humanity — then we must all have divine potential. We must be God-bearers — called to incarnation, called to compassion. I believe that our fundamental spiritual nature ultimately impels us to connection. It is the only way we will come to say no to hunger, to rape, to murder, to disease, to violence of all kinds. It is only when we sink into the divine within that we ourselves become conscious of being a little bit of God. When that consciousness happens, we must truly begin to love one another. We must long for peace as we touch into our own deep inner peace (God). Ultimately, we recognize that we *are* one another and intricately connected. It is then that we ourselves will become the ones who will save the world — a scary thought, but one that can only remind us of the words of Jesus: "Greater things than these you will do."

It will be a long journey, but it has already begun. Many who have experienced loss, displacement, and suffering are already aware of the new and deeper spirituality that moves within like a hunger that must be fed. This hunger impels us to healing, to wholeness, and a deep compassion for our earth and all living things. It leaves us in awe at the oneness to which all of us are called. It is the beginning of wisdom, and an awareness that all have a place and a purpose to be honored and respected in the universe. The human race is moving into a new and profound spiritual space as we ponder, Who and where is God? The answer to that lies deep within us.

Part II

Building Community

The Ecclesial Challenge

10

God Is the Question
and God Is the Answer

Sandra M. Schneiders

Writing about the "most important spiritual question of our time" in a *Festschrift* honoring a woman who has written so much and so well, so challengingly and so courageously, on the burning questions of our day, is a task more than a little intimidating. In her writing and speaking Joan Chittister has confronted racism and poverty, misogyny and patriarchy, violence and war, homophobia and xenophobia, ecological destruction and genocide, and numerous other issues, each of which can lay some claim to being the most important of our time. I can hardly hope to match the scope of her concern or the quality of her response.

Furthermore, the very qualifier, "most important," raises questions about the question. Are we talking about the important or the essential? Equal rights for women in the church is crucially important, but the radical dismantling of patriarchy, only one of whose pernicious manifestations is the oppression of women, is essential, not only to the life of the church, but for the future of the human race. Are we talking about the important or the urgent? International economic justice is enormously important, but a bowl of food, today rather than tomorrow, is the most urgent concern of many people in sub-Saharan Africa, as is shelter from subzero weather for the homeless on our streets. And then there is the question, important for whom? For the east or the west, the north or the south? For whites or people of color? For women or for men? For the human race or for the cosmos as a whole? For the privileged or for the poor? For believers or nonbelievers?

As I reflected on the complexities of the assigned question, I found myself backing into it by asking a mirror question: What is the major problem today? Is there anything common to all the disturbing, tragic, violent situations that overwhelm us? And conversely, is there anything common to all the sparks of hope that keep us going? Unoriginal as it may seem, the response that kept repeating itself in my mind and heart was that the central problem, the besetting struggle at the heart of all our issues, is the life-and-death battle between the self and "the Other." And the most enduring source of hope is the capacity of some people for genuine self-transcendence, for selfless preference of the Other, sometimes at the cost of life itself.

The most destructive force at work in our world, it seems to me, is not scarcity or natural disasters or historical mistakes. It is the centripetal force at work in the heart of every one of us that wants to draw everything we touch to ourselves. Certainly greed — the voracious appetite for the latest, the best, the most, the different, the convenient, the expensive, the private, the easiest, the most impressive — underlies the obscene consumerism of the American lifestyle and the corresponding desperate poverty of so much of the rest of the world. Is it not narcissism that makes commitment to costly, large-scale social causes and involvement in the survival of the people in our own neighborhoods seem too complicated or too time consuming? Cocooning in our comfortable "lifestyle enclaves"[1] is justified by our sense of unavoidable busyness, or the pseudo-belief that taking care of our own will insure that the good life will "trickle down" to the less lucky, or even the sense of not being responsible for the misfortune of others, which, after all, we did not cause. The deadly anger that fuels the death penalty advocate's demand for "emotional closure" that can come only through vengeance on those whom one cannot and will not forgive contributes to an endless cycle of violence. It moves from the vindictive individual to the punitive state and church to the warmongering nation that will brook no opposition to the export of its self-serving economic dynamics at whatever cost to the subjugated nations. The need to dominate and control, if not eliminate, those who are different from oneself rather than learning to respect and value the Other, the desire to protect one's turf from those who would share power or participate in deciding their own fate, keep patriarchy in the church, neocolonial exploitation of "underdeveloped" and indebted countries, domestic violence and child abuse, rape, racial oppression, homophobia, and xenophobia virulent in our culture. Our conviction that everything exists, or at least should be made to serve, our good, our comfort, our convenience, justifies the ecological violence and prodigious waste that eliminate species by the thousands, pollute our land, water, and air, and destroy the resources upon which the next generation (to say nothing of the next seven generations) depends.

The underlying dynamic of all these destructive patterns and behaviors is a deep-seated inability to transcend the self, to choose the good of the Other above one's own, to "lay down one's life," actually or figuratively, in small matters or in great, for those we love. Perhaps, even more fundamentally, it is that we cannot disentangle ourselves from our self-concern enough to love those outside our own circle of relations and friends. We are really incapable of that selfless movement that is the unique glory and dignity of the human being.

On the other hand, when a ray of light penetrates the darkness of human self-absorption, it invariably comes from the life of someone, like Nelson Mandela or Dorothy Day, like Theresa Kane or Raoul Wallenberg, like Mother Teresa or Bede Griffiths or Simone Weil, who have risked security, reputation, the comfort of familiar surroundings, and even life itself to make a difference in a world of oppression and violence.

It seems to me, as I have reflected on the paralyzing inability of so many of us to really prefer the Other to ourselves, not just in theory or desire but in actual practice, that the only basis for such self-transcendence is the recognition of a value that does not compete with the self. For who or what, finally, can compete with my own sense of value, my own instinct of self-preservation, my own need to have and be all that I can be in the one and only life I will have to enjoy, but is ultimate in a sense I cannot claim to be, even to myself? Only something that so relativizes my self that it awakens me to the genuine value of the Other as an autonomous center of subjectivity, that does not derive from or reflect upon me, can pull me out of the quagmire of self-absorption into the radiant light of other-centered love. Only something that truly transcends me, that is evidently the only real Center of the universe, is capable of decentering me and therefore relating me appropriately to everything else. Only from such a decentered point of view can the Other truly come into focus, not as an extension of, a support for, an annoyance to, or a competitor with myself, but as an equal who makes a claim upon me that is as important as my claim to be the center of my universe. The only such value, finally, is Love, the infinite self-giving outpouring of goodness that Christians recognize as God, for "God is love, and those who abide in love abide in God, and God abides in them" (1 John 4:16).

This brings me to the answer, or at least to my answer, to the question posed for this essay. The most important spiritual question of our time, it seems to me, is the God question. Is there a God, and if so, what is God like? Is there anything, Anyone, who can call us beyond ourselves in respect, love, and service of the Other, not as an object of our patronizing superiority or even our generous benevolence, but as a genuine claimant on our very humanity? If yes, then we cannot be ultimately fulfilled as persons unless we are engaged in making life, happiness, and fulfillment possible and real for all those with whom we share existence and life in this fragile cosmos.

Given the length restrictions on this essay and its likely readership, I will presume an affirmative answer to the first part of the question, even though I know that it is not at all self-evident to many of our contemporaries that God exists and that the engagement of atheism and agnosticism is a major theological responsibility of our time. My concern is with the second part of the question: What is God like? Although we may be tempted to assume that all Christians agree on at least the broad outlines of the answer, the issues in the daily news evidence radical disagreement among believers about what God is like. Creationists and evolutionists, fundamentalists and liberals, death-penalty advocates and opponents, pacifists and just-war advocates, and people taking a variety of positions on the many issues mentioned in the paragraphs above, especially when they appeal to religious warrants for the positions they take, have very different versions of God, even if they belong to the same religious tradition or denomination.

It seems to me that, while there are certainly all shades of diversity around the question of what God is like, most images of God are built up in response to two questions. First, there is the question of whether God is ultimately transcendent in the sense of being outside, above, unaffected by all reality other than "himself," or whether God is ultimately immanent, so deeply interior to all reality that God cannot be imagined as separate, outside, or distant.[2] Is God's transcendence what separates us from God or is it what plunges us into God, making us "participants of the divine nature" (2 Pet. 1:4), "friends of God, and prophets" (Wis. 7:27)?

Second, there is the question of whether God is ultimately the human male writ large, the divine "Marlboro man," the dominant, powerful agent bending all to "his" unaccountable and nonnegotiable will, and reflected best in the exercise of authoritarian power to crush all dissent and opposition. Or is God most truly Holy Sophia, divine wisdom immanent in all that exists, "reaching from end to end mightily and ordering all things sweetly" (Wis. 8:1), who is best imaged as a feminine, life-giving presence luring all creation forward into the fullness of life and being?[3]

Theologians today, especially those working from within a feminist framework, are struggling mightily with this question,[4] which is not a purely theoretical issue to occupy the minds of underemployed academics. Who God really is determines what we, made in God's image and likeness, are called to become. Our response to the questions that confront us most urgently today is a function of what we believe about the kind of ultimate value that underlies all reality, including ourselves. The relation of humans to the rest of creation, so long modeled on the image of a dominative deity, can change only if that divine sanction of absolute human sovereignty is finally undermined. Only an inclusive God who effectively wills the salvation of all can guide us toward the kind of nonrelativistic religious pluralism that will delegitimate forever the mentality as well as the practice of the Inquisition, both inside and outside the church. If the privileged are ever to recognize that their gifts are not a right to more than their share, but a responsibility to the less fortunate among their equals, their sisters and brothers with whom they share in God's unbounded parental love, it will be because that divine parent no longer appears as a patriarchal paterfamilias with a preference for the firstborn male, but as the infinitely loving source of all life.

My conclusion is that the most important spiritual question of our time is whether there is anything, any value, finally, Anyone, who can claim our whole heart and thus wrest us free of ourselves so that we can be and live for one another. I suspect that all our wandering and experimenting must lead us finally to the only answer that will not disappoint or betray us, individually or as a human family: God is the question and God is the answer. Better still, God is the mystery in whom we live and move and have our being (Acts 17:28), whose true nature and intent were revealed to us in a human being, Jesus of Nazareth, who freely laid down his life for the Others, for us whom he chose to call not servants but friends (John 15:13–15).

Notes

1. This expression was coined by Robert Bellah in his classic work on American individualism, *Habits of the Heart: Individualism and Commitment in American Life* (Berkeley: University of California Press, 1985), 72.

2. This issue was thrust into the center of theological discussion in the 1960s by panentheists in general and process theologians in particular and has been carried forward by feminist theologians.

3. For a good synthesis of the Old Testament material on the feminine personification of God as Holy Wisdom, see Roland E. Murphy, *The Tree of Life: An Exploration of Biblical Wisdom Literature* (New York: Doubleday, 1990), 133–49. Elizabeth Johnson shows the relevance of the figure of Wisdom for our understanding of Jesus in "Jesus, the Wisdom of God: A Biblical Basis for a

Non-Androcentric Christology," *Ephemerides theologicae lovanienses* 61 (1985): 261–94.

4. See, for example, Elizabeth A. Johnson, *She Who Is: The Mystery of God in Feminist Theological Discourse* (New York: Crossroad, 1992); Catherine Mowry LaCugna, *God for Us: The Trinity and Christian Life* (New York: HarperCollins, 1991); Sallie McFague, *Models of God: Theology for an Ecological, Nuclear Age* (Philadelphia: Fortress, 1987).

11

The Questions That Liberate New Life

Diarmuid O'Murchu

Joan Chittister has written and lectured extensively on religious life. Her analysis of our current situation is insightful and provocative. Frequently she alludes to our diminished numbers, few vocations, dwindling apostolates, yet her analysis always effuses a sense of hope. Her vision is refreshing and her enthusiasm for the future is inspiring and contagious.

Her analysis of religious life outlined in *The Fire in These Ashes* will continue to engage and inspire women and men religious for many years to come. That book also inspires in other ways, succinctly unearthing some of the great cultural and spiritual questions of our time. I use one quotation from the book to explore the question that titles this essay. In my opinion, it is one of the great visionary statements bequeathed to us by Joan Chittister.

In *The Fire in These Ashes* we read, "The religious voice must be the voice that brings to the public debate the best in tradition, the finest in theological analysis, the keenest in social perception and the most challenging of gospel values."[1] Although addressed specifically to those in the vowed life, the statement invites us all to consider what we bring to the table of dialogue in today's world. It invites us to think big and to think inclusively. And we are challenged to bring what is deep and ancient in all our sacred stories, whether personal or cultural.

New Horizons

In adopting this quotation for the reflections that follow, I wish to suggest the most important spiritual question of our time is about *enlarged horizons of meaning*. Traditional constructs, religiously sanctioned or otherwise, no longer appease the seekers of our time. Conventional parameters, whether religious, social, or political, do not liberate truth but rather stifle and stultify creativity. New horizons are beckoning us from every sphere of contemporary life. We need new eyes and reawakened hearts to discern this call of our time.

Joan Chittister offers us four fertile guidelines. She suggests that we need to reclaim anew (1) the best in tradition, (2) the finest in theological analysis, (3) the keenest in social perception, and (4) the most challenging of gospel values. I propose to explore briefly the visionary implications of each of these.

What Tradition Are We Talking About?

On the face of it, *tradition* seems an ordinary and harmless word. We often allude to our historical, religious, and political traditions. In African countries people speak liberally of the tradition of the elders. We are often reminded of the need to safeguard and preserve tradition; occasionally, we are challenged to reappropriate our traditions. Joan invites us to reclaim *the best in tradition*. That is quite an onerous task, one that requires us to shed many anthropocentric and patriarchal assumptions. For example, when Christian theologians use the word, it tends to be about the events of Christian history, particularly of the past two thousand years. For scientists, it covers a time span of about five hundred years, dating back to the rise of classical science in the sixteenth century. And for historians — and here is my major concern — it applies to what is popularly called "the rise of civilization" in the Sumerian culture of five thousand years ago.

All these expositions of tradition beg more questions than they answer. When we suggest that civilization spans no more than five thousand years we are automatically asserting that everything that happened prior to that time was uncivilized, barbaric, primitive, prelogical, savage, and so forth. We are setting ourselves up as anthropocentric judges, dictating that reality can be only what we suggest it should be. In the process we are condemning ourselves to personal and cultural ossification. Scripture scholar Walter Brueggemann describes it as a state of cultural amnesia. We are a species without a story because we have cut ourselves off from our long evolutionary tradition. We live in the fabricated world of forced forgetfulness. Little wonder that spiritual writers and psychotherapists have a heyday in helping us to deal with our alienation. In most cases they are only exacerbating the predicament.

There are several strands of tradition that we need to reappropriate. Today, cosmology is surfacing as the supreme wisdom of our time, connecting us anew with the marvel of the cosmos we inhabit. All the religious traditions affirm belief in God's participation in the creative, evolutionary process right from the beginning. When are we going to take this belief seriously? When will we choose to discard the anthropocentric idols of formal religion that often distract us from engaging with the co-creative God whose revelation to us is billions of years old?

Perhaps, we could begin to do it if we at least reclaimed our own sacred tradition as a human species. Paleontologists inform us that we humans have inhabited the Earth for over four million years, and there is growing evidence to suggest that for much of that time we were highly creative creatures. Some one hundred thousand years ago, after thousands of years of symbolic interaction with the sounds of nature, we evolved human language; some seventy thousand years ago we buried our dead with distinctive religious ritual; forty thousand years ago our artistic potential took a quantum leap (Ice Age Art). Why do we ignore so much of our sacred story? Why do we collude with such destructive reductionism? Why do we treat our past with such ignorance and disrespect?

And what do we make of religious tradition? Each of the major religions considers its own story (revelation) to be the whole truth, in the face of which all others are perceived to be somehow inferior. In a culture of multifaith dialogue we try to be tolerant and nonjudgmental, but we are evading crucial issues. The tradition of mainstream religion — itself about five thousand years old — is largely a development of patriarchal consciousness, a ploy to exert control over human creativity. The deeper truth of all religion is rooted in a much more ancient spiritual unfolding and the endowment of creation itself flourishing for billions of years before humans ever evolved. We are spiritual creatures because the creation out of which we evolved is itself spiritual. Over the millennia we have incultured this spiritual inheritance in a vast repertoire of "religious" expressions, all of which have been culturally conditioned. I suggest that formal religion needs to be viewed within this larger context.

Critics are quick to retort that this attempt at historical retrieval (for which there is minimal factual evidence) is nothing more than a "New Age" fixation about a long-lost golden age. I am not in pursuit of a golden age of any description. My concern is the evolutionary story of the human species, and my conviction that the creative Spirit of God was at work in that process from the very beginning. Why then do we focus religious attention on the past five thousand years and consign to oblivion the remaining 95 percent of our sacred story?

The consequences of our impoverished story I consider to be enormously destructive; the personal, social, planetary impact has been one of debilitating alienation and a great deal of meaningless suffering. To rediscover *the best in tradition* requires a great deal more than historical and cultural retrieval. There are significant theological factors, to which I will now turn attention.

Theology: The Expanded Horizon

Joan Chittister invites us to bring to the table of dialogue *the finest in theological analysis.* Traditionally, Christian theology claims to be based on the deposit of faith as contained in sacred Scripture. In recent decades we have stretched that understanding to include insights from other religions and from the wider spiritual traditions of humankind. What precisely the subject matter of theology is today is itself a keenly debated topic.

Thomas Aquinas adopted Anselm's notion that theology was about "faith seeking understanding," with faith understood officially as the deposit of faith. Today, however, we know that several people pursue a search for faith, but not within the context of formal religion. Anselm's guideline may be strangely relevant to our time, as long as we are prepared to work with this expanded understanding of what we mean by "faith" — what Karl Rahner one time called "the subject's openness to the unlimited expanse of all possible reality in which we are fundamentally drawn toward an ever transcending horizon of absolute mystery."

However, it is not the content of theology that pushes new horizons today, but rather, the people who do theology. Prior to 1960 the study of theology in the Catholic church was reserved to priests and students studying for priesthood; only males could study theology. Slowly, and with no conscious effort on anybody's part (as far as I am aware), this monopoly was broken, and from 1970 onward laypersons, females as well as males, began studying theology. And by the end of the 1970s a substantial number of laypersons were teaching theology, especially in the United States. It is estimated that by the year 2010, 60 percent of all theologians in the Catholic church will be laypersons, and three-quarters of them will be women. For the first time in the history of Christendom the clerical monopoly on theology will be broken. This may well be the single greatest revolution happening in the Catholic church today.

There are several implications to this development, one of which I single out for attention. As laypersons take over the pursuit of theology, and become confident in doing so, the subject material will also change quite dramatically. Already we are witnessing a focus on the major questions related to the world, attributing a diminished importance to questions pertaining to the church. The new generation of theologians theologizes around the perennial questions of our time: human rights, ecology and environment, medical ethics, "third way" politics, economics for justice, liberation from all forms of oppression, and the furtherance of right relationships at every level of life.

In terms of the Christian "deposit of faith," there is a waning interest in who Jesus was or is (divine or otherwise) and a growing commitment to what Jesus signifies for our world — the vision of the new reign of God, the *basileia*. Gradually, but irreversibly, theology is moving out of the sacred canopy of formal religion right into the heart of the world. It is becoming what perhaps it was always destined to be: the people's own supreme wisdom, expressing a sense of faith that responds to God at the heart of creation rather than merely assenting to creedal formulations.

To do the "fine analysis" that Joan Chittister suggests will require of the theologian of the future a multidisciplinary, systemic base. Wisdom based on many fields of learning will be required, and where this is not possible for the one person (which will be the majority of cases), then theology is destined to become a team enterprise! Where all this will leave formal church and religion is a concern on which few can offer a clear prognostication. Current indications are that questions of perennial spiritual significance will continue to be explored — possibly more outside the church than within it!

Our Breadth of Vision

When Joan Chittister writes about *the keenest in social perception* she is inviting the reader to that contemplative space out of which she has lived and ministered for over forty years. The contemplative gaze tends to be lateral and profound, and something of a rare quality in today's world, especially in the sphere of formal religion. In words reminiscent of the great Thomas Merton, Joan describes contemplation as "the ability to see through, to see into and to see despite, to see without blindness. It is the ability to see a whole world rather than a partial one."[2] Contemplation is all about perception, not so much of God as of God's work in the fabric of creation. It is the vision that is open to originality, surprise, challenge, being disturbed; to question, to explore, to wonder, and above all, to proffer an alternative vision to the stereotyped and stultified perceptions of our imperialistic culture. While the world today is being swept along by an information revolution, wisdom is a scarce commodity. It is only the wise in heart who can see the deeper meaning, the delusion of language, and the ideology of rhetoric.

Our world now, and always, is in urgent need of fresh namings, more wholesome understandings, and enlarged horizons. The journey to truth is a perpetual pilgrimage in search of authentic perceptions. In Joan's own words, "When the filter through which we see the world brings us to openness and compassion for that world — humility in the face of it, vulnerability to the impact of it, nonviolence in dealing with it, and respect for its otherness — then creation is recreated, and humans become human again."[3]

Christianity: Central Values

Ever since the adoption of Christianity as the religion of the Roman Empire, the values of imperialism have dominated Christian belief. This co-option led to an abdication of the liberating vision of the new reign of God, quickly replaced by a model of church characterized by power, domination, control, and legalism, coupled with a subservient holiness, in which the participants are often described as "children" and occasionally referred to as "slaves." With the contemporary church facing impending disintegration, the gospel vision of the new reign of God calls us anew to grow up and become adult witnesses to our faith. Engagement in the mission of Jesus is about relationships of love and justice requiring adult participation in a world of adult people. It requires a quality of relating, resilient and tough, passionate and compassionate, addressing issues of daily import in a real earthly and cosmic world.

Incarnation does not belong to the patriarchal God who requires a quality of childlike submission and subservience from obedient and loyal servants. Incarnation is about engagement with all the resources of one's being with the co-creative God who co-creates with us, humans (and with all other creatures), in bringing about a world order, a worthy abode in which the new reign of God can unfold and flourish.

Wisely, indeed, Joan Chittister challenges us to reappropriate *the most challenging of gospel values,* to outgrow the congested world of ecclesiastical holiness (with its many noble and heroic achievements of the past), and to embrace more fully the call to be agents for that love, justice, and liberation which belong essentially to building up the new reign of God at the heart of creation.

The Most Important Question

North American theologian Mary Daly suggests that a great deal of Western discourse is characterized by "drooling and droning." Empty words, bombastic rhetoric, and broken promises no longer placate the hungering masses. Our empty stomachs (well over half of humanity) and our emptied-out imaginations (largely the work of formal education) drive us to ask questions we have never asked before. Cynicism and skepticism abound. Yesterday's answers carry neither weight nor conviction. The culture of postmodernity has largely abandoned the search for answers. Unfortunately, in its compulsive drive toward deconstruction, it fails to surface questions that would facilitate a fresh search for hope and meaning. In the covert and liminal spaces of our culture, where people search for new ways forward, important questions surface on a daily basis. Central to this pursuit is this question: As we strive to arise from the ashes of patriarchal demolition, what are we meant to be about as a planetary and cosmic species?

In sum, we are meant to be about encountering God where God first encountered us: not within a specific culture, religion, or church, but in those planetary and cosmic engagements where evolution pushes open the creative horizons of the Spirit, who blows where she wills. Prophetic people like Joan Chittister inhabit these enlarged horizons; they open pathways, alluring and risky. It is in the interest, not just of church or religion, but of creation at large, that many more forsake the safe havens of bygone days and embrace this bold adventure of the faith that characterizes our time.

Notes

1. Joan Chittister, *The Fire in These Ashes* (Kansas City, Mo.: Sheed & Ward, 1995), 144.
2. Joan Chittister, *Womanstrength: Modern Church, Modern Women* (Kansas City, Mo.: Sheed & Ward, 1990), 51.
3. Joan Chittister, *Heart of Flesh* (Grand Rapids: Eerdmans, 1998), 175.

12

"The Hint Half Guessed, the Gift Half Understood, Is Incarnation" (T. S. Eliot)

Richard Rohr, OFM

Joan, I want to say that you have given me courage to ask about the important spiritual questions of our time, and sometimes to try to address them. You, like Yeats's falcon, keep circling around the essential questions, while also diving into them with immense courage and clarity. Whatever I might try to say here is informed and freed by your persevering wisdom. Thank you dearly, good friend.

Since I can dare to speak only for the Christian contribution to the immense world of spirituality, and since I believe Christianity is meant to serve as "salt and leaven" in the world and not an exclusive club for the saved, I believe we need to name our gift very precisely, very modestly, and also very courageously. Christianity must stop asking and answering the merely theistic question and begin to offer its unique and irreplaceable gift: incarnation, embodiment, integration. "Here the impossible union," says T. S. Eliot.

With always wonderful exceptions, Christian history has largely served to prop up the world of religion for the European and Mediterranean mind and their colonies. It has allowed itself to offer the needed God figure with an available Jesus, to prop up nations' needs for social order and control, to sacralize patriarchy, to bless wars and cultural pretense, and to turn Jesus who said "Follow me" into a pedestalized and insecure god who seems to be shouting "Worship me." This is not even close to the gospel, and yet it seems to be most of what we were capable of in our early, probably infantile, period of two thousand years.

Our protected and defended religious images are still largely cultural, devotional, costume, and ritual. People seem willing to identify with liturgical symbols much more than with the indwelling presence, the essential image, that must be seen and honored — at the cost of major conversion — in all creatures. Too much emphasis on tribal and culturally trapped images only gets in the way of the great and necessary seeing. We circle the wagons around a very tiny body of Christ (an oxymoron, it seems), when the goal is the great body of Christ, the enfleshment of God once and for all and forever and everywhere. Could anything smaller be a victory for God?

In general we have tried to establish the vertical pole of theistic religion: the sacred, the transcendent, the otherworldly, the sanctuary, the clergy, the moral and compelling mandates that we need to hold together. It has served many good purposes. For one, it frees us from our false maps and our always egocentric, small selves. It is good religion, but not gospel. It is only half of the picture, and not yet the unique revelation of Christianity. Jesus is saying something else and something more. He tells us not just of a God out there, but the great and perfect surprise that God is perfectly hidden and perfectly revealed within here. He horizontally hides the whole thing so cleverly that only the mystics and the sinners have discovered either the language or the experience: those who listen well and those who lose well seem to get to the empty tomb first. The rest of us seem to be content to blow incense into the sky.

Maybe human consciousness itself had to be readied for the mystery of incarnation, maybe science had to be ready to back it up, maybe we had to experience the negative results of a vertical and dualistic worldview, maybe this is the real meaning of "the second coming" of Christ, but I believe that we will soon put the human and the divine together as precisely and profoundly as Jesus did in his historic Jewish body. Then maybe we will cease to exploit the physical world, rape the human world, and addictively consume the sensual world searching for Spirit. Transcendence-out-there leaves you split and unsatisfied, and immanence without transcendence leaves one addictive and compulsive because it is not true and you always have to up the dosage to try to satisfy, but transcendence-within-here leaves you peaceful, content, and energized. Suddenly, the now is enough, the here is good, the this is godly, the Image is everywhere, and the soul is satisfied. The world is one, so is God, and so are we.

I am told that the first thousand years of the Christian era spoke of the human species as the *corpus verum,* the true body of Christ, and the eucharistic bread as the *corpus mysticum,* the mystical body of Christ that fed and named the real body. Ironically, the use of the terms reversed in the second millennium, and now we speak of the Eucharist as being the "real presence" and the gathering of God's people as being the "mystical body of Christ." It seems to me that the earlier intuition was clearly closer to the revealed mystery. History, like the Bible itself, seems to be three steps forward and two backward. How else could we move toward the Absolute?

Perhaps we backed off of it when we recognized its massive implications for human relationships, personal dignity, penal systems, war, politics, economics, religion, and liturgical practice. That was far too much to reinvent and reimagine in two thousand years. Human consciousness can hardly bear that much mystery, that much holiness, that much of God set loose in the world. It is much easier to hold God in tabernacles, bow down before defined places, keep reality split and safe and piously sacred, than to believe in what was revealed in the oh-so-human body of Jesus. We would just as well sew the temple veil back together. We like the sacred and the profane in easily distinguished compartments. It leaves us looking like we are on our knees, but utterly in control — of God.

Suddenly, we might not need a cultic priesthood, and lay baptizers might start pouring water for the forgiveness of sin down by the riverside. Suddenly we might have to honor the earth, animals, and others as the epiphany of God. We might have to stop killing old men and infants with impunity. We might have to kiss the feet of foreigners, sinners, and other religions instead of the easy kiss of golden crosses. We might have to put our sexuality and spirituality together in one place and one person instead of leaving them split and sedated. Who wants all of this? This is a new place where none of us knows how to live. No — you are right — you are not there yet. Me neither. I only want to be. But we are being led, and irreversibly led.

The tangent is clear, the teaching is hidden in plain sight, the Spirit is stirring, the goal of incarnation is inevitable. It will indeed be the second and full and final coming. Be honest — what else would be gospel, good news? What else would hold it all together? What else would be more than we asked for or dared imagine? Maybe I can dare to use my brother John Duns Scotus's simple "proof" for the Immaculate Conception here. He said, "If it is fitting, and if it is possible, then God will do it." We call it the mystery of the body of Christ, the communion of saints, the divine indwelling, the incarnation, the eternal enfleshment of God in Christ. We grasp to name such a mystery from every side, but the words always seem rarefied and distant until it happens in us.

Let me end with a quotation from my favorite mystic, Julian of Norwich. It is no surprise that we forgot her and lost her for several hundred years. She was literally "unthinkable" for most of Christian history. Listen to her daring words:

> We are all one in God's intention ... and Jesus said to me most comfortingly, "I may make all things well, and I can make all things well, and I shall make all things and I will make all things well; and you will see for yourself that every kind of thing will be well ... " and in these five words God wishes us to be enclosed in rest and in peace. And so Christ's spiritual thirst will have an end. For this is Christ's spiritual thirst ... to gather us all here into him, to our endless joy. For we are not now so wholly in him as we then shall be.[1]

Later, she seems to call this God's "Great Deed," which none of us dared to imagine: God shining through the physical creation in all its forms. Perfectly hidden, yet once said, perfectly obvious.

It is now for those who can see. It is not yet for many and for me. But it is, and it is everywhere, and it is enough. I and many, many others thank Joan Chittister for being a postmodern Julian, who again teaches what none of us are ready for but all of us want, and because of her, many of us believe.

Notes

1. Julian of Norwich, *Showings,* trans. Edmund Colledge, OSA, and James Walsh, SJ (New York: Paulist Press, 1978), 229–30.

13

Seven Monks Invited to Honor
Joan Chittister

Mary Lou Kownacki, OSB

Ryokan: Prophet

When Ryokan wrote,
"Oh, that my monk's robe
Were wide enough to embrace
The suffering of the world"
He was invited
To recite before the king
And handed a poet's crown.

My bet:
If Ryokan pounded
On the emperor's palace gates
And from his monk's robe poured
    An eighteen-year-old boy maimed in battle
    A hungry child with empty rice bowl
    Prisoners on death row
    Missiles of mass murder
    Women with bound feet and tied tongue
Then Ryokan becomes
A dangerous revolutionary
And is hanged by royal decree.

Synclectica: Spiritual Guide

Amma, great desert mother,
women gathered at your feet
listening.

"Amma, duc verbo."
Amma, give us a word...
to make us whole

And from your lips leapt
a sun so afire — flames of blinding light,
of burning love ignited

the darkest and coldest
corners of self. A fire, we blazed
into cathedrals, castles, the center of cities.

Li Po: Visionary

Legend says that Li Po,
Young hermit of Min mountain,
Rode home on the back of an eagle
Drinking richest wine from the Tao.

Legend says that Li Po,
Drunk in a boat,
Fell into a river and drowned
Trying to embrace the moon.

In the Great Smokies last night
Overlooking Lake Douglass
I saw Li Po,
Whiskey in hand
Dancing on yellow waves
Hosting a poetry slam with Great Blue Heron.
"My life a blaze of spent abundance," he chanted
With toothless grin, raising a toast,
An invitation to die
Reaching for what you cannot.

Hildegard of Bingen: Leader

Don't keep it a secret.
Hildegard was put under interdict
for refusing to exhume
a friend buried in her monastery's cemetery.
Abbess Hildegard narrowed her gaze
at church fathers
who said the dead man's sins

spewed bile through blessed ground.
This is my jurisdiction
said Hildegard, the Greenness of God.
Everywhere I look, juicy rich grace.

Merton: Writer

I pass the pen. The stacks of paper
scribbled with dashed dreams
of a monastic life alive. Beneath the cowl
blazing eyes to pierce the wall of lies
passed from cloister and Rome and bishop throne.

I pass the pen. The stacks of paper
scribbled with dashed dreams
of monastic life alive. Beneath the robe
a heart broken by war, cries of the poor,
a gospel word spoken too late for fear of State.

I pass the pen. The stacks of paper
scribbled with dashed dreams
of monastic life alive. Beneath the scapular
my hands writing word by word a message I hear
to breathe green into dead bones, find bread in stones.

Scholastica: Mystic

How can I possibly sleep
And miss the morning star?
Come, brother Benedict,
Let us light incense
And chant the sutra

Awake,
Totally aware,
My knees turn weak
From God's long, open-mouthed kiss.

How can I describe Your presence:
A dab of precious perfume
Behind my left ear.
All day long Your scent intoxicates me.
How others are drawn to nibble
On my ear!

Hotei: The Enlightened One

Hurry, the enlightened one
Enters the city gates,
An old patched bag slung over a shoulder.

The enlightened one
Meets a hungry child
Reaches into the bag and bread appears.

In a golden carriage a bishop approaches.
A lightning bolt escapes the bag and strikes
Him to the ground. I'm blind, he cries.

Long lines of women gather
And tongues of fire fly from the bag
Into their mouths. They speak with new voice.

Representatives of the state appear
Armed for battle. Truth topples from the bag
And strips them naked.

An old woman pulls at the enlightened one's robe,
Tears streaming from her eyes. Out of the bag
Comes a listening heart.

Oh, for that bag you should sell everything.

14

Guess Who's Missing at Dinner

Kenneth A. Briggs

The pulpit of my snug boyhood church commands a large place in my memory from the pew where my scrawny frame rode low; it loomed like the prow of an oncoming sailing ship as viewed from a rowboat in its path. The preachers who occupied that white wooden perch, swathed in severe black robes, supplemented those dimensions, investing that pulpit with an authority that has remained with me. From on high the Word was delivered unto us.

The preacher's voice verily shook the shoebox country sanctuary with lessons from the leather-bound King James Version, from the foibles of Eden to the psychedelic terrors of Revelation. Apart from the hope of the Gospels, nothing arrested my attention more than the alarms and the comforts of prophesy. The urgings of Jeremiah and Ezekiel, Isaiah and Joel, Daniel and Jonah, and many others stirred dread of judgment and promise of liberation. God was unhappy with the desolation and misery we had inflicted on our fellow human beings, but at least God *cared,* and it mattered to God how we treated the poor (confession: I translated certain of these admonitions into ways in which my parents could improve their custody of their children and ardently hoped they would do the same). Faithfulness meant doing God's work of justice and mercy. That message lodged in my heart, both haunting and inspiring, and endures no matter how far I wander from heeding it.

As I experience these times, I don't find much tolerance for those legendary scolds and barely any tolerance for what they were trying to tell us. No doubt Habakkuk long ago resigned himself never to becoming a household word, but, worse, the prophetic tradition itself has been banished to the religious and secular fringes. This tragic circumstance cries out for redress. Prophets have always been unwelcome intruders into our comfortable, self-satisfied dwellings, of course, but they seem unable to get even a foot in the door in our self-congratulatory times. The most acute challenge before us, I believe, is to invite these God-obsessed, sacred mouthpieces into our midst, no matter how scruffy or blunt-spoken, to deliver that troubling and reassuring Word anew. As I write this, I am grateful for Joan Chittister's stubborn insistence on keeping her door wide open.

We especially need prophets now to remind us that God's will far surpasses the search for personal wholeness and the gospel of wealth. We have been drowning in self-absorbed religiosity, invoking all sorts of divine names and incantations to rid ourselves of emotional and physical illness caused largely by the pathologies of a consumer-driven society. Rather than apply the prophets' analysis to these sources — materialism, competition, greed, idolatry — we have settled for a frenzied effort to fix the victims of this maelstrom who have succumbed to its insanity. Or on the other hand, we have devised other "inner" means to enable the winners in this grand game, the "successes," to feel good about themselves by justifying their largesse on grounds of individual merit or by easing them into a state of inner serenity where, it is supposed, it is possible to live unto oneself. The theology reads as such: God further helps those who help themselves by maximizing their contentment.

There is little wonder that the prophetic word has been shut out of this climate. In a culture whose citizens salute the economic model of free enterprise as the one true holy creed, everything else is expected to become subordinate and supportive. Religion can be the prophetic resistance but rarely has chosen that role. To some extent and in some places, the prophetic Word fired up believers to combat slavery, to pursue civil rights, and to oppose the Vietnam war, but that flurry was fleeting as it was powerful. Mostly, and increasingly, religion, with a few notable exceptions, has bent to the cause of free enterprise by refraining from a moral critique of big business and by equipping workers with religious-sounding incentives needed to keep the market humming. The record is spotty at best on all fronts. The Catholic church, for example, eventually did endorse the union movement, to the raves of the prophets, I suspect, but the bishops have apparently heard little from the prophets more recently on the host of worker injustice matters. Religion has been satisfied, for the most part, to retreat into privacy to care for individual souls. Robert Bellah's classic, *Habits of the Heart,* has given an unmatched picture of this headlong race toward religious subjectivism.

I am cautious about making this into an inner-outer dichotomy. The inner life has certainly been neglected and needs nourishing. There is nothing inimical about the relationship of inner and outer. To the contrary. An authentic prophet in Jewish and Christian traditions is grounded in prayer. The old Christian disciplines that have been dusted off and reintroduced recently have restored meaning to countless lives and reoriented them to God. None of that should be minimized or dismissed. The inner journey can indeed save the lost and heal the broken — all of us, that is. I am also aware of St. Paul's powerful body of Christ imagery, the most beautiful case for organic diversity ever made. Just as the human body needs a multitude of different parts — hands, ears, feet, and so forth — so the Christian body needs a variety that includes the gifts of teaching, comforting the sick, and prophesying. In the analogy, no part or no function is superior to another, but all perform separate tasks. Together they enable the whole body to function as it should. None makes sense without the others. Each part values the others equally and considers all indispensable. Detaching healers or teachers from prophets and ministers to the sick does violence to the body of Christ. In effect, the church has done that by severing the prophetic mission from the mission as a whole. The body has been divided into discreet tasks, some highly valued, others, like the deeds of the prophet's cry, dismissed as peripheral.

When I hear some spiritual seekers speak of putting their own lives together, I can only be thankful that they have received this gift of grace. Whether or not these seekers have the gifts of prophetic mission, I also hope that they would recognize and support those who do bear that mission and that the seekers would receive the blessings of the prophets. Sadly, that kind of mutuality seems rare. The pursuit of individual salvation has not spawned an appreciation of the causes of mercy and justice in the wider, outer world. No, it has contributed to a church consumed with inwardness. A valid quest has turned into a reckless binge.

Inwardness has detached us from the oppression that surrounds us. It has given us a truncated version of spirituality that, by omission rather than commission, tells us that the crimes of structure, the pathologies of corporate and political exploitation, lie beyond our competence and capacities as spiritual beings. Our aim is perfectly worthy: to be serene and good. The danger is that such an aim has so often become reductionistic. It is a moral meltdown process that holds that practicing religious ethics boils down solely to conducting personal relationships in accord with sound moral precepts. Questions of whether one should support a union drive at Wal-Mart or figure out the implications of ethnic profiling or rethink capital punishment largely fall almost completely outside the circle of ethical concern. Between the totally private and the totally worldly is the realm of "family values" that constitutes an exception of sorts. Certain of these issues — abortion, school vouchers, prayer in the schools — border on a wider frame of reference, but only with regard to these select matters of belief and ethics. It doesn't invalidate any of these campaigns, but it does illustrate the clear limits of ethical involvement. Thus, the American Catholic bishops have fought abortion but muted, at best, their opposition to the death penalty, even after the pope denounced the practice during his trip to St. Louis. Even family values issues get muddied. For all their lofty preachments on the integrity of parent-child bonds, for example, the bishops were unable to act, even a little prophetically, by insisting that the Cuban boy, Elian Gonzalez, be returned to his father. Could fear of speaking out, of losing Cuban-American support, have kept them quiet?

The determining factor is what the spiritual authorities are believed to want from their followers. H. Richard Niebuhr, the Reformed theologian who taught at Yale, defined five ways various Christian groups related to their cultures based on their picture of how Christ did so. At one extreme was Christ against culture, expressed by churches that removed themselves from society; at the other, Christ and culture, whereby churches simply blessed the culture and melded into it. Much of the current "me and God" spirituality somehow manages to embrace both.

The rubber-stamp option reflects the highly conformist streak that has been thoroughly converted by the success ethic and its payoffs. Even those who don't participate in it give it their uncritical blessing. The danger, of course, is that the prophet has been exiled. The results can be frightful, as they were in Nazi Germany. The German churches (again with notable exceptions) fell into quietism during the Third Reich, endorsing the creeping chain of events or at least failing to think it was their business. Any direct analogy would be wrong. Fascist Germany is not democratic America. Our religious culture has seen fit in recent memory to take the mantle of Jeremiah to combat racial injustice and a war in Southeast Asia. The dynamics of this huge smorgasbord of religious communities is too diverse and too powerful to expunge all prophetic utterance. But, all the same, we are in a quietistic mode that has shriveled our notions of what spirituality means. The entrenched creed of this culture is economic. The oppression that results is also economic — and, of course, racial and political. There is no comment to speak of.

Niebuhr's other extreme, the sect mentality that sees itself as living out Christ's separation from culture, has also found resonance in our time. The religious community that sees itself as ministering predominately to the "spiritual needs" of its people often becomes a kind of religious therapeutic center concentrated in upon itself. While it may pose as an alternative to the culture, standing apart from the culture's wicked ways, it is prone to be fully accepting of the culture's major economic and political creeds. So it's the old "each one save one" individualism and collective spiritual consumerism, more or less. In Niebuhr's typology, it is the best of two worlds: an attitude of separatism, the benefits of conformity. The walking wounded from that world out there are patched up and sent back into action. Fortunately, Niebuhr had among his other options the "conversionist" Christ who is perceived as working with the prophetic community to transform the structures of an unjust culture.

This morning's paper carried a story that read in part, "Blacks routinely receive longer sentences than whites in Pennsylvania even when their crimes and prior records are nearly identical, an Associated Press review of thousands of state sentencing records found." Until such matters become central spiritual concerns, we are missing something vital. As we do so, we do well to remember that the form in which prophetic messages are contained means as much as their content. Unless those who purport to convey God's message are themselves embodiments of God's purposes, it will be for naught. Prophesying is more than shouts of anger and denunciation and threat. It is at bottom an expression of God's love.

Abraham Joshua Heschel, the great Jewish thinker, wrote stirringly about the prophets of the Bible who helped ignite his own social justice activism. (Who could ever forget the diminutive, bushy-white-bearded Rabbi Heschel marching across the perilous Selma, Alabama, bridge at the head of the line next to the Rev. Martin Luther King Jr.?) "The prophet is a person, not a microphone," he wrote in volume two of *The Prophets*. "He is endowed with a mission, with the power of a word not his own that accounts for his greatness — but also with temperament, concern, character, and individuality. As there was no resisting the impact of divine inspiration, so at times there was no resisting the vortex of his own temperament. The word of God reverberated in the voice of man."[1]

Heschel continued, "The prophet's task is to convey a divine view, yet as a person he *is* a point of view. . . . We must seek to understand not only the views he expounded but also the attitudes he embodied: his own position, feeling, response — not only what he said but also what he lived; the private, the intimate dimension of the word, the subjective side of the message."[2]

In Heschel, we come full circle. Prophesy is public, but its authenticity derives from the subjective integrity of those who practice it. The outcry against outward structures requires inward certainty. It is all spiritual, whether we know it or not. This, it seems, is our lesson. Our society, our love of comfort, wealth, peace, and personal harmony with God have warped our capacity to understand the crucial, spiritual role of the prophet.

From a pulpit similar to the one from which I, in my itchy wool Sunday suit, had first heard the promise that justice would roll down the mountain like a flowing stream, a veteran executive of the World Council of Churches once declared that as he got older his theology became more conservative and his social outlook more radical. How could he take the Gospels seriously, he reasoned, without accepting the implications for a more just world. The two sides, theology and social ethics, were in conversation, as they should be but so seldom are. One influenced the other. I would hope that in coming years the spirit would invite the prophet to a full share of conversation.

Notes

1. Abraham Joshua Heschel, *The Prophets* (New York: Harper & Row, 1962), xii.
2. Ibid.

15

We Just Don't Get It

Robert F. Keeler

In the long annals of persistent denseness, the continuing inability to get it, the first disciples of Jesus rank high. But are we any better?

Repeatedly, Jesus had to endure the frustration of knowing that they just didn't understand. In the Gospel narratives he seems barely able to contain his exasperation as they take the wrong meaning from his words, or snooze through key events, such as the transfiguration and the agony in the garden.

Now, two thousand years later, we see the first disciples as lovable knuckleheads, but we don't realize how much we are like them. Like those disciples, we love Jesus as our wise teacher, as our great brother, as the incarnation of our compassionate God. But when he speaks, sometimes we seem to be catching a few winks — like Peter, James, and John on Mount Tabor and at Gethsemane — and often we just don't get it.

We still fail to apprehend one crucial element of the message of Jesus: nonviolence. Mohandas Kharamchand Gandhi, one of the greatest peacemakers of this or any other century, offered this appraisal of Christianity: "The only people on earth who do not see Christ and his teachings as nonviolent are Christians." If he were speaking in the language of today, he might have added, "Duh! Hellooooo?"

To me, this centuries-old denseness poses the most important spiritual question of our time: What will it take to make all Christians return to the nonviolence of the gospel?

Somehow, those early followers of Jesus came to understand this issue well. The original disciples failed to understand much of what Jesus was telling them, but after the Lord's death and resurrection, followed by the powerful wind of the spirit at Pentecost, the first generation of Christians began to get it.

One of the texts they absorbed with particular care was the Sermon on the Plain, reported in Luke 6. In that discourse Jesus pronounced these difficult words about nonviolence: "Love your enemies, do good to those who hate you, bless those who curse you, pray for those who abuse you. If anyone strikes you on the cheek, offer the other also; and from anyone who takes away your coat do not withhold even your shirt."

The earliest Christians heard those words and reflected on the actions of Jesus, actions that clearly rejected violence, even if violence could have saved him from the horrible torture of crucifixion. So they, too, rejected violence — even to the extent of avoiding military service in an empire that made overwhelming military power almost a sacrament.

One influential leader of the church at Rome, Hippolytus, proclaimed that no one who had embraced professional killing should be received into the faith. No Christian should volunteer for military service, Hippolytus argued, and if drafted, Christians should refuse to kill.

Eileen Egan has written, "The early witnesses, martyrs, bishops, priests, teachers, and laypeople, all agents of transformation through their transformed lives, had achieved a revolution of peace and nonviolence in hearts and minds.... There followed a revolution in the other direction. The new revolution brought the followers of Jesus to an acceptance of violence and warfare."[1]

The turning point in that new revolution was the year 312, when Flavius Valerius Constantinus, on his way to becoming the Roman emperor Constantinus, Constantine the Great, thought he saw a vision of a cross in the sky. The vision held out the promise of victory at the pivotal Battle of Milvian Bridge if he would fight under that banner. Unfortunately for all Christians for all time, Constantine won. The following year, after Rome had persecuted the church for almost three hundred years, Constantine's Edict of Milan proclaimed Christianity an official state religion.

From that dark era until this very hour, the poisonous embrace of the state has smothered us. From that time on, Christians have willingly served in Caesar's legions. Even today, Christians happily supply not only the soldiers to slay in the name of the state, but the chaplains to wear crosses on their military uniforms and bless the bloodshed.

One of the most famous chaplains of all was the late Cardinal John J. O'Connor of New York, who served for twenty-seven years in the armed forces of the United States, the only nation in history to drop nuclear weapons on another nation. In 1999, not many months before his death, he demonstrated publicly that even a much beloved archbishop can fail to get it.

The issue that attracted his attention was sex. A young male Air Force officer, stationed in one of the intercontinental ballistic missile silos that still flourish like wheat in the Great Plains, was worried about sexual temptation. His job required him to spend long hours in a small, confined space with one other officer. That officer happened to be a woman, and he feared that she might become for him an occasion of sin. So he wanted a different assignment. Moved by the young man's vigilance against the dangers of the libido, Cardinal O'Connor wrote two newspaper columns supporting him.

Nowhere in any of the newspaper stories about the young officer's concerns, and nowhere in Cardinal O'Connor's columns, did the underlying reality of the officer's duty assignment arise. Every day, he had to be ready to help launch a missile that could instantly incinerate millions. If the officer saw his job itself as sinful or an occasion of sin, that did not appear in the stories. Nor did Cardinal O'Connor reflect publicly on the possibility that the willingness to destroy millions of distant lives might somehow be more sinful than impure thoughts.

Cardinal O'Connor was a great man, with many fine qualities. He was a strong voice for the poor, a champion of the rights of working people, an outspoken foe of abortion, a major force in the Catholic-Jewish dialogue, as much mourned in the Jewish community as he was in the Catholic. Toward the end of his life, he even began questioning some uses of military force. Like so many Christians, however, he fell into the lingering Constantinian error that poisons our church: the embrace of the state and of military service.

This episode of sin and the silo is a clear example of our flawed moral vision. We have taken a radical message about justice for the oppressed, the imprisoned, and the hungry, a message about non-violence and love for the enemy, and turned it into a message mostly about sex. Yes, our bishops do oppose capital punishment, and many of them strongly criticize the use of military force, but collectively, they only pump up the volume and communicate forcefully on the sexual issues.

For nearly seventeen hundred years too many of us have been ignoring the wisdom of the earliest Christians, the men and women who could still hear the words of Jesus echoing in the Galilean hills, who could still feel the bracing breeze of Pentecost, before Constantine's vision began to change everything.

The words of the Sermon on the Plain are still there. But we have marginalized them. We have taken those stark and unequivocal words, "Love your enemy," and construed them as merely an impossible ideal that we can safely ignore.

As we hear these words, we simultaneously translate the word "enemy" and downsize it. We envision an enemy whom we could possibly imagine loving — an annoying uncle, perhaps, to whom we haven't spoken for years, or a football rival. That must be the enemy Jesus meant. He couldn't possibly have been thinking, for example, about Saddam Hussein.

Similarly, we have heard the admonition to turn the other cheek and the prescription in Matthew 5, "Do not resist an evildoer." We have decided that this teaching would only make us passive doormats, waiting in fear for the bullies of the world to beat us up. But we are missing the point.

"When the court translators working in the hire of King James chose to translate *antistenai* as 'Resist not evil,' they were doing something more than rendering Greek into English. They were translating nonviolent resistance into docility,"[2] Walter Wink wrote in a brilliant analysis of the nonviolent resistance that Jesus actually did advocate.

"Jesus did not tell his oppressed hearers not to resist evil," Wink wrote. "That would have been absurd. His entire ministry is utterly at odds with such a preposterous idea. The Greek word is made up of two parts: *anti*, a word still used in English for 'against,' and *histemi*, a verb which in its noun form (*stasis*) means violent rebellion, armed revolt, sharp dissension....A proper translation of Jesus' teaching would then be, 'Do not strike back at evil (or, one who has done you evil) in kind. Do not give blow for blow. Do not retaliate against violence with violence."[3]

In other words, Jesus saw that the cycle of violence is endless, creating generation after generation of reflexive enmity and insatiable bloodletting, but solving nothing. So he advocated fighting evil, but using neither passivity nor violence. His third way was the way of militant nonviolence. It is a way that, sadly, we have too seldom tried. We just don't get it.

But Mohandas Gandhi got it, and his militant nonviolent resistance brought independence to India. If we wonder what the creatively nonviolent third way of Jesus might look like in practice, we have only to study Gandhi's salt march.

The Rev. Martin Luther King Jr. got it, and his nonviolent movement began the long, painful process of introducing equality to a nation that had preached it for two centuries but had practiced something quite different.

Archbishop Oscar Arnulfo Romero got it, and his courageous, eloquent resistance to the death squads in El Salvador provided the seed of ultimate liberation.

In contrast, President Bill Clinton, reacting to the Columbine High School shootings by urging the nation to find ways to curb violence while he was at the same time leading the NATO bombing in Kosovo, doesn't get it.

Unfortunately, the president is not atypical of Christians in America. We do not speak out unequivocally against violence, as the first generation of Christians did. Rather, we accept state-sponsored violence as the inevitable way of the world — in the execution chambers, in the skies over Iraq and Kosovo, in the perpetuation of obscenely high military budgets that strangle spending on the real needs of people.

Violence even follows us into the voting booth. In 1992, for example, we had a choice between President George Bush, whose Operation Desert Storm led to a million deaths, or Governor Bill Clinton, who made it a point during the presidential campaign to approve the execution of a developmentally disabled man. My own ballot solution was simple: I wrote in the name of Sister Joan Chittister. She's been a great president for me: no scandals, no bombing raids, no violence.

In fact, what we really need in our times is a lot more Joan Chittister and a lot less Bill Clinton. We need prophetic voices who are willing to call us back to the insight of the earliest Christians, that following Jesus means embracing nonviolence.

We need to look carefully at the way we have allowed our allegiance to Caesar to dilute our fidelity to the gospel. We need to look at the American flags in our churches, so omnipresent that we don't even notice them, and be shocked at this intrusion of the state into the sanctuary, just as the Rev. Albert Nolan, the great Dominican theologian from South Africa, was astounded on his recent visit to America. Even at the Church of the Holy Sepulchre in Jerusalem, perhaps the most sacred shrine in Christendom, I experienced unconscionable coziness with the dominations and powers: at the end of an otherwise acceptable liturgy the organist played "The Star-Spangled Banner" as a recessional hymn!

We need to reject the facile doctrine of TINA (There is No Alternative) and return to the nonviolent alternative that Jesus proclaimed. We need to reclaim the wisdom of the church's founding fathers and mothers, who rejected violence, no matter what it cost them. We need to make it as unthinkable for a Christian to enlist in the armed forces or serve as a military chaplain as to work in an abortion clinic.

We Christians are supposed to be a countercultural force, a counter to the pervasive violence of our society. How do we recover that prophetic, pre-Constantine witness? For me, as we leave behind the bloodiest century in human history, that is the most important spiritual question of our time.

Notes

1. Eileen Egan, *Peace Be with You: Justified Warfare of the Way of Nonviolence* (Maryknoll, N.Y.: Orbis Books, 1999), 41.

2. Walter Wink, *Violence and Nonviolence in South Africa: Jesus' Third Way* (Santa Cruz, Calif.: New Society Publishers, 1987), 13.

3. Ibid.

16

Toward a Spirituality of Communion

Richard P. McBrien

The most important spiritual question of our time is also the most important spiritual question of any time: How does one live in communion with God, under whatever name — the Holy, the Sacred, the Transcendent, the Wholly Other, Being? For Christians, that question has been essentially modified by the coming of Jesus, by his invitation to discipleship, and by the distinctive spiritual dynamic he proclaimed, embodied, and fulfilled in his own "passing over" through self-sacrifice and death to new and eternal life.

What Jesus taught us is that communion with God is achieved through communion with one another and with the whole created order — a communion, in other words, that is not only individual but communal, and not only personal but cosmic.

At the core of Jesus' preaching and ministry is the reign, or kingdom, of God (Mark 1:15). One can inherit the reign of God only through love of one's neighbor (Matt. 5:38–48). Indeed, the whole of Jesus' preaching and teaching was concentrated in the one commandment of love: the love of God and the love of neighbor, with the latter being the expression and proof of the former (Mark 12:28–34; Matt. 22:34–40; Luke 10:25–28; cf. 1 John 4:20). On this one commandment the law and the prophets depend (Matt. 22:40). Among the many and diverse implications of this commandment are that we should not presume to offer sacrifice to God unless and until we have been reconciled with our sister or brother (Matt. 5:23–24), nor should we presume to ask God's forgiveness of our sin unless we are also ready to forgive those who have sinned against us (Luke 11:4; Matt. 6:12).

Nevertheless, it would be wrong simply to equate love of God with love of neighbor. Religious acts that establish or strengthen the bond of communion with God, such as liturgical and private prayer and various forms of contemplative and mystical experience, pertain more directly to the love of God than to the love of neighbor (Matt. 6:1–15; 7:7–11; Mark 14:38). On the other hand, "religious" access to God through prayer, mystical and otherwise, can never completely be divorced from the principal sacramental encounter with God in the neighbor. The great picture of the Last Judgment in the parable of the sheep and the goats (Matt. 25:31–46) offers one of the classic illustrations of this principle.

To be sure, entrance into the reign of God is not conditioned solely on one's love of neighbor. Jesus announced that "the time is fulfilled, and the kingdom of God has come near," but he added that one must first "repent, and believe in the good news" (Mark 1:15). In his hearers' minds, repentance would not be a matter of making an act of perfect contrition and "going to Confession," but would consist of a fundamental reorientation of one's whole life, of changing one's whole outlook on reality and establishing new patterns of thinking and behavior based on that new outlook.

This repentance and conversion experience demanded also a belief in the gospel of forgiveness that Jesus preached (Mark 2:5, 10, 17). He drove home his point with various parables, especially those in Luke 15, the parable of the prodigal son in particular. Jesus was so committed to the forgiveness of sins in the name of God that he made himself the friend of outcasts — the publicans and sinners of Matt. 11:19 — and did not avoid their company (Mark 2:16). Indeed, he rejoiced over their conversion (Luke 15:7–10; Matt. 18:13).

For Jesus, the antithesis of a repentant attitude is one of self-righteousness and presumption. He repudiated the proud Pharisee (Luke 18:9–14), the elder brother who resented his father's benevolent reaction to the prodigal son's return (Luke 15:25–32), and the discontented laborers in the vineyard (Matt. 20:1–15). He said that publicans and harlots would enter the kingdom of God before those Jews who thought themselves better than everyone else (Matt. 21:31–32), for God, he said, will exalt the humble and bring down the proud (Luke 14:11; 18:14). Each of us must pray that God will forgive our sins just as we have forgiven the sins of others against us (Luke 11:4; Matt. 6:12).

Jesus' message was not given only to faceless crowds as he moved from place to place. He deliberately gathered disciples around himself, encouraging them to leave home, and indeed everything else, take up their cross, and follow him (Mark 1:16–20; 2:14; Luke 9:57–58; 14:26–27). Thus, Jesus advised the rich young man who asked how he could become his disciple first to sell all that he had and give the money to the poor (Mark 10:21). In other words, the call to discipleship is a call to the imitation of Jesus himself (John 13:15). The disciple is to act like Jesus: with compassion, humility, and generosity, and as the suffering servant of others (Mark 9:33–50; 10:41–45). This love for others, as an expression and proof of one's love for God, is the distinctive and essential mark of Christian discipleship (John 13:34–35). Such love, however, is not to be reserved for one's family and friends. The disciple is also commanded to love the enemy (Luke 6:27–28), to renounce revenge (6:29), to avoid judging and condemning others (6:37), and to be careful not to dwell on the speck in the neighbor's eye while missing the plank in one's own (6:41–42). Everything is summed up in Paul's classic hymn to love: "And now faith, hope, and love abide, these three; and the greatest of these is love" (1 Cor. 13:13).

The love of God and the love of neighbor, and all that each implies, are not possible without the gift of the Holy Spirit. Indeed, the Holy Spirit is *the* gift of Jesus to his disciples (Acts 2:38; 8:17–20; 10:45; 11:15–17; Heb. 6:4), and it is given not just to an elite few but to the whole community of disciples (Acts 1:15; 2:1–3). It is a gift that enables the disciples to "live according to the Spirit" (Rom. 8:5).

Spirituality, in the end, is a comprehensive term that pertains to our way of being transcendently human, that is, of living a fully human life that is rooted in the life of God. To be spiritually human is to live by a higher principle, rather, by the highest principle, which is Being itself. God is the principle of personal, interpersonal, communal, and even cosmic transformation. To be "open to the Spirit" is to accept explicitly who we are and who we are called to become, and to direct our lives accordingly, in response to God's grace (presence) within us. Christians name that Being God, and name the reality of God's relationships with us as Father/Creator, Son/Redeemer, and Spirit/Sanctifier. It is the life of the Holy Spirit that incorporates the Christian disciple into the body of Christ, the church, and through whom the Christian has access to God the Creator in a life of faith, hope, love, and service.

The spiritual challenge for our time, and indeed for all time, is somehow to maintain a proper balance among, and a dynamic integration of, the essential "ingredients" of any authentic Christian spirituality. For reasons given already, this spirituality must be at once trinitarian, christocentric, pneumatological, and eschatological. But it must also be visionary, sacramental, relational, and transformational. It is visionary when it incorporates the new way of seeing reality (the fundamental notion of repentance, as we have seen above) and of seeing through things to their spiritual core, of thus "interpreting spiritual things to those who are spiritual" (1 Cor. 2:13). It is sacramental insofar as it is based on the conviction of faith that everything is imbued, to one degree or another, with the hidden presence of God and is thereby a potential instrument of God's saving activity on our behalf and the world's. It is relational because we are by definition relational beings — beings in relation to God, to one another, and to the world. To be human is to live in community, just as to be Christian is also to live in the community that is the church. The relational character of Christian spirituality requires a sensitivity to the presence, the needs, and the gifts of others, as well as to the created goods of the Earth. Finally, Christian spirituality must be transformational, that is, always open to the presence of the Spirit as a power that heals, reconciles, renews, gives life, bestows peace, sustains hope, brings joy, and creates unity. An authentic Christian spirituality — for our time and for all time — requires that the Spirit be allowed to work in us and in others so that, through the instrumentality of the individual and of the church, the transformation of the world into the reign of God might continue to occur.

Although there is only one Spirit, there are many different spiritualities, even within the church itself. As we seek to define the core and challenges of Christian spirituality for our time and for all time, we need to be guided by certain basic theological principles:

1. We are body-spirits, not spirits somehow imprisoned in our bodies. A spirituality that depreciates the body and sets the body and the spirit in some kind of dualistic tension is not a spirituality for our time or for any time.

2. We are radically social beings. No Christian spirituality, for our time or for any time, can lapse into an individualism that ignores our connection with one another and with the wider natural and cosmic orders.

3. We are individual subjects, that is, distinct centers of consciousness and freedom. Even though we share a common humanity with others and a solidarity with the whole created order, we remain unique individuals, with our own distinctive experiences of God. As such, no Christian spirituality, for our time or for any time, can impose itself as the only Christian spirituality.

4. We are graced. The presence of God enters into the very definition of who we are as humans. We are created by God, elevated and redeemed by Christ, re-created by the Holy Spirit, and destined for eternal glory. No Christian spirituality, for our time or for any time, can be based on a repression of our humanity as if there were something essentially corrupt or dishonorable about it.

5. We are sacraments of God. Indeed, all reality has a sacramental, or mysterious, character. God is present to the whole of created order, animate and inanimate alike. No Christian spirituality, for our time or for any time, can prescind from creation and the environment we inhabit. In the spirit of Ignatius of Loyola, a Christian spirituality, for our time and for all time, strives always to see God in all things.

6. We are destined, along with creation itself, for the final reign of God, a kingdom of justice and peace as well as of holiness and grace ("Pastoral Constitution on the Church in the Modern World," no. 39). No Christian spirituality, for our time or for any time, can ignore the demands of justice, peace, and human rights, or be indifferent to the needs and cries of the poor, the powerless, and the marginalized.

7. We are sinners. Accordingly, there can be no authentic Christian spirituality, for our time or for any time, that is fashioned independently of the cross and of the constant need for repentance and forgiveness. It is a spirituality marked by sacrifice and by denial, not so much of the flesh as such, but of selfishness. It is ever on its guard against the counterforces of pride, apathy, temerity, lust, hypocrisy, sloth, and envy.

8. We are ecclesial persons. There is no authentic Christian spirituality, for our time or for any time, that is not rooted in the liturgical, sacramental, and devotional life of the church. It is a spirituality activated and nourished by the preaching of the Word and in particular by the celebration of the Eucharist, which the Second Vatican Council referred to as the summit and source of the whole Christian life ("Constitution on the Sacred Liturgy," no. 10).

9. We are called to be virtuous persons. An authentic Christian spirituality, for our time and for any time, is rooted in, and is a lived expression of, the theological virtues of faith, hope, and love; of the cardinal virtues of prudence, justice, fortitude, and temperance; and of the related virtues of humility and gratitude, of mercy and concern for the poor, of forgiveness and truthfulness, and of stewardship for the environment.

10. The call to holiness is a universal call ("Dogmatic Constitution on the Church," chap. 5). An authentic Christian spirituality, for our time and for any time, is not multitiered or hierarchical — one set of levels for the elite (priests and sisters, monks and nuns, brothers) and another for the laity. Every baptized Christian is called to perfection, whether ordained or not, whether religiously professed or not, regardless of gender, race, ethnic background, or social and economic

status. We are all one in God through Christ by the power of the Holy Spirit.

How one achieves that communion with God and with one another, and indeed with the whole of God's creation, is, always has been, and always will be the most important spiritual question of our time.

17

From Asia with Love

Thomas C. Fox

As I type, I am looking out a window over some congested streets below. Traffic extends in four directions — and it is not moving. The intersection is in gridlock. A brownish-red haze hangs overhead. It is hot, muggy, and has not rained for days. The sidewalks are crowded, people darting between small stands where vendors sell soup, fried meats, and vegetables. Most seem to be ignoring the beggar who sits cross-legged, his head down, his right arm extended. I am in Bangkok, Thailand.

I was here thirty years ago and remember these streets. At that time a war raged in Vietnam. It taught me the arrogance of power and the enduring strength of Asian ways. There were few cars then, no congestion, little pollution, and elephants commonly walked these streets. Bangkok today is a sprawling city of more than five million, and it is said to be slowly sinking into the mud.

I am in an air-conditioned hotel room. It has a television connected to a satellite on the roof. I count twenty-two channels, five in English, including CNBC and CNN. On MTV several British women sing and dance in tight blue dresses adorned with white feathers. I turn the channel to the *Asian Market Hour,* where a young analyst explains that U.S. interest rates are unlikely to rise and as a result Asian stocks are likely to remain stable. He advises to keep an eye on electronic stocks. Two Thai channels broadcast beauty contests featuring heavily made-up contestants who lack the grace and charm of the women selling vegetables outside my window.

I am in Thailand for a once-every-five-year gathering of the Federation of Asian Bishops Conferences, or FABC. The ten-day meeting drew some two hundred bishops, theologians, and Asian lay leaders to a large pastoral center about thirty miles outside the city. Thirty years ago rich vegetation dating back seventy to one hundred million years grew on the land surrounding Bangkok. Today the drive from central Bangkok to the pastoral center takes one through endless rows of concrete commercial and residential buildings. It is part of what we have commonly come to understand as urban sprawl.

Rainforests are being destroyed at a staggering rate. According to the National Academy of Science, at least fifty million acres a year are lost, an area the size of England, Wales, and Scotland combined. All the primary rainforests in India, Bangladesh, and Sri Lanka have been destroyed already. The Philippines lost 55 percent of its forest between 1960 and 1985; Thailand lost 45 percent of its forest between 1961 and 1985. Despite the small land area they cover, rainforests are home to about half of the five to ten million plant and animal species on the globe and support ninety thousand of the 250,000 identified plant species.

From the outset the bishops insisted that all their reflections must stem from the social, political, and economic context in which they are found. Bangkok screams context. This largely Buddhist nation, home to some three hundred thousand Catholics, is being ripped from its traditional moorings by demographic pressures, new technologies, and changing global economic forces. The Asian bishops talk about the spread of violence growing out of extremist fundamentalism. They say that this is part of a larger Asian unease and an attempt to hang on to a past they see slipping away. The bishops stated, "We are aware that 'cultural globalization' through the over-saturation of the mass media is quickly drawing Asian societies into a global consumer culture that is both secularist and materialistic, undermining or causing the erosion of traditional, social, cultural and religious values that have sustained Asia." The bishops see this process leading to "incalculable damage."

At the conference they also stated, "We are committed to the emergence of the 'Asianness' of the Church in Asia. This means that the Church has to be an embodiment of the Asian vision and values of life, especially interiority, harmony, a holistic and inclusive approach to every area of life....For the whole world is in need of a holistic paradigm for meeting the challenges of life."

Six weeks before the dawn of the new millennium, Pope John Paul II traveled to New Delhi to address the Asian bishops. He said that "just as in the first millennium the cross was planted on the soil of Europe, and in the second on that of the Americas and Africa, we can pray that in the third millennium a great harvest of faith will be reaped in this vast and vital continent." What he had in mind is the spreading of the message of Jesus as Savior across the continent of Asia during the next thousand years. The Asia bishops prefer to use other words, speaking of witnessing the faith and dialogue. At the end of the papal address, Cardinal Julius Darmaatmadja of Jakarta, Indonesia, responded to the pontiff, saying, "Yes, it is true that there is no authentic evangelization without announcing Jesus Christ as Savior of the whole human race. But for Asia, there will be no complete evangelization unless there is dialogue with other religions and cultures. There is no full evangelization if there is no answer to the deep yearnings of the peoples of Asia. There is no convincing and trustworthy announcement of Jesus as the Savior, unless along with, or even preceding this announcing, the church presents the actual loving ministry of Jesus which rescues people from situations of injustice, persecution, misery, and in the place of these brings life, yes, even life in abundance."

I left my two weeks with the Asian bishops hoping that the third millennium will be an Asian millennium, if it means the growth and spread of the varied Asian values throughout the world. I see the churches of Asia as experiencing a kind of Pentecost. These churches are young, idealistic, and energetic, and they are gaining the confidence they need to develop their Asian roots. The bishops of Asia talk about "a new way of being church." They see their churches building communities and working with the other religions of Asia to face the moral and ethical challenges of the day. They talk about a triple dialogue with the other religions of Asia, with local cultures, and with the poor. Their vision builds on the multiethnic experiences that comprise Asian ways and lead to emphases on tolerance, compassion, and harmony in the support of life.

The mystics of East and West have long taught that all that is seen and unseen is part of an essential whole. They embrace all as sacred, starting with a sense of the sacred within. The West has been slow to grasp these notions. Too often we live with blinders and therefore miss the wonder and awe of creation. Rediscovering the sacredness of life, of all creation, is, in my opinion, the spiritual challenge of our time. The many injustices, acts of inhumanity, wars, and assaults on nature with which we are so familiar grow out of a kind of spiritual blindness. The dawn of a new millennium offers us a unique moment, perhaps a final reprieve, to reconnect us with the Spirit of Life. This moment provides the possibility of a planetary awakening. That many voices are articulating these visions is a sign of hope. That they are coming to life in our church is a special blessing. Pray that we be open to the Spirit.

Part III

Transforming Structures

The Global Challenge

18

Confidence

A Way to Be Human

Ivone Gebara

A response to "What is the most important spiritual question of our time?" is certainly a personal one, and it carries within itself plural questions and responses that have origins in many different human groups. I will try to sketch a response from the Latin American view and more particularly from the view of northeastern Brazil, where I live and work.

For me, one of the most serious spiritual questions of the world today is the lack of confidence of the human person in the human person. This statement appears to be paradoxical and contradictory when we see the scientific and technological advances of such great importance in evidence around the world. Aware of these advances, we should have more confidence in ourselves and in our capacity to solve problems. Because of them, we should be able to believe in our ability and the illumination of our reason, which is capable of offering responses to the different problems that arise. We could imagine that there would be a sharing of knowledge and material goods for the happiness of all groups of people at least in proportion to the growth in intelligence and awareness within the human heart. Growth in the area of ethics could at least keep pace with scientific and technological learning. However, it is not so. At times I have the impression that our scientific and technological advances only underline the profound crisis of confidence that human persons have in themselves. Spiritual growth is profoundly out of step in relation to material and intellectual growth.

This lack of confidence translates into forms that are varied and concrete. Among the poor we see that the abandonment in which they find themselves many times develops into mechanisms of violence as a means of survival. As life seems to have no value, survival becomes everything. Violence in the barrios of the poor, disputes between the various groups living there involving such things as drug trafficking, is shocking. In this environment of injustice and total lack of protection religious movements proliferate that, at first glance, offer support and security. However, after some time we see how they alienate the poor from their rights and the historical responsibilities that are theirs. This does not mean that popular movements struggling for their rights without religious connections do not exist. But in these as well, this lack of confidence in the human person is present. Never have we walked in so much darkness, feeling our way, as if we do not "see the invisible" in the realization of our hope. Many other groups find themselves assaulted by the same "sickness" of lack of confidence and lack of concrete hopes. I personally feel this very strongly in the social movements in which I participate and the movements of the church.

Patriarchal and hierarchical structures seem to have grown stronger in Latin America at the end of this century. We cannot forget that Latin America is the largest Catholic continent in the world and is in a privileged place in the hopes of the Vatican. It is a place where the religious "market" is growing and where competition for members follows the "free market" logic. Religion appears one more time to be a symbolic force of public expression only capable of supporting injustices, not combating them. Faith is reduced to an intimate expression with exterior manifestations of celebration. Prophecy is forgotten and silenced. Public denouncements are few. Confidence in our own capacity is alienated in favor of the authority of charismatic religious leaders considered capable of "leading" the people.[1] This charism as "guides of the people" does not translate into ethical contexts, but rather is used for the gathering of large prayer groups that lose themselves in a popular delirium of constantly repeated phrases and expressions of praise. Loud songs and dances are the preferred expressions of the new Christian religion. A public, individualistic catharsis takes place that gives the participants the impression that they have encountered "god" in their subjectivity. Everyone feels happy, mixing smiles with tears in their worship, which consists of pleas for assistance. Everything appears beautiful and problems are forgotten for the moment.

I believe that the lack of confidence of the human person in the human person is the "work" of our hands. Greed, the destruction of nature, the elimination of different human groups, silence in the face of multiple aggressions, failure to act in the face of cultural structures oppressive to women and children, impunity, and any number of other things in this line lead us to the sickness in which we find ourselves today. The human fabric is being corroded by "moths" that are given birth from within ourselves, especially within those who hold economic, political, and religious power. The will to destroy or radically transform this corrosion has not yet grown within us. We feel badly, we feel threatened, but we continue as "humanity," still relying on social models that are exclusive, believing that the privilege and the well-being of the minority can be guaranteed to the detriment and unhappiness of the majority. We continue maintaining a hierarchical religion that exaggerates the masculine and enslaves the feminine. We continue to esteem its divine wars and its high priests dressed in red and purple, dancing on stages and resting on satin beds. It seems that reactions are few, that we believe that the power of these religious leaders comes from God and that they are representatives of the true ideal of Christianity.

Who will return to us our confidence in ourselves? Who will wake up our hearts to perceive "the other" as being in our own image and likeness? Who will awaken us to perceive that we are part of the Sacred Body? Who will announce the "good news," that which continues to ask us to prepare our paths of justice and kindness for all people?

I ask these questions within the basic question that directs this reflection. To ask the most urgent spiritual question leads me necessarily to ask the most urgent questions around the material. We note that humanity is one indivisible unity, articulated and interdependent in relation to all that exists. We perceive, then, that the big spiritual questions are the big material questions, and the big material questions are the big spiritual questions. If greed is of the spirit, the object of greed is material goods. Excessive consumerism and the possession of material goods reveal within themselves a sickness of the spirit. They reveal our inability to be satisfied with what is basic so that there may be life with dignity in which all human groups have the right to participate. They reveal our inability to see the other as sister and brother or simply like ourselves. The others are still enemies who threaten us, and for this reason we need to create means of protection against them, or even eliminate them.

Our collective illness is so serious that it leads us to an undue appropriation of the food, drink, land, and culture of the others. We fail to see the others and their needs, in order to dominate them. Thus, what is important is the need and the desire of the strongest, or those who judge themselves to be the strongest. We hide from the "certainty of death," and try to make it disappear even though it is always present. We act as if the earth and its riches will always be and that it exists for the use of the "well born" minority.

We women have lived a long history of hiding in society and the Christian churches. We are slowly coming out of this situation, showing ourselves publicly, expressing our thoughts. This process of "unhiding" is extremely diverse and unequal in different countries. In Latin America we are still very far from the "unhiding" of women of the Christian churches. Religious institutions present themselves publicly with masculine authority even though feminine participation is by far the largest in number. Masculine domination continues to present itself as strong even though we know that the masculine is weakening and losing its hegemony. Feminine dependence is explicit, at least for those of the official church. Once again, religion appears as a "place of alienation" for women, a place where their social and political minority status is accentuated and glorified in favor of the continuity of masculine domination. It is here that we again find ourselves faced with the "sickness of the spirit" that expresses itself in the lived reality of unequal systems of human relations and alienating organizations of power structures. The spirit of submission and dependence is a sick spirit, a state contrary to the call to liberty contained in the depth of all human beings. And the religious Christian institutions seem to contribute to this sickness of the human spirit.

One more time I return to the question: Who will help us find paths of salvation?

I believe more than ever that salvation is already in the midst of us in different manners. It is enough to be attentive, and we will perceive that the dream of justice and solidarity continues to live in different places on the earth. It is necessary only to believe that this salvation will be capable of fermenting the human mass and producing much fruit in solidarity, kindness, and justice.

This salvation present among us is expressed in different political, social, cultural, and religious movements that insist that we do not have to adapt to the "words of the order" of the system in which we live. Salvation comes to us from the spontaneous groups that organize here and there to help others, to denounce injustices, and to manifest public solidarity with the needy. Salvation is manifested in the public word and in the texts written by so many women and men who do not tire of repeating the need to have a "heart of flesh," a heart of compassion for all people and all the Earth.

In the midst of so many prophetic and saving words, words that are whispers and breezes of hope among the strident noises of the thousand and one wars, is the ministry of Joan Chittister. Her writings cross lands and seas and nourish the hope of many beyond the boundaries of our nationalities. I am proud to be one of the beneficiaries of her gentle and powerful word. I am happy to belong to the same community of people who are passionately in favor of life, a community to which she belongs and that goes beyond any congregation, church, or religious creed.

Translated by Katia O'Reilly, OSB

Notes

1. I refer to the growth of neo-Pentecostal Catholics and Protestants. They take up more and more space in the media and present themselves as the answer to the anguish and hopes of the people. See, for example, no. 74 of the periodical *Epoca,* São Paulo, October 18, 1999.

19

Passion for God,
Passion for the Earth

Elizabeth A. Johnson, CSJ

The image of our planet Earth from space, a blue marble swirling with white clouds, has become familiar to this generation. Astronauts whose own eyes have seen this view speak of its power to change their deepest feelings and attitudes toward the world. Saudi Arabian astronaut Sultan bin Salman al-Saud, part of an international crew, recollected, "The first day we all pointed to our own countries. The third day we were pointing to our continents. By the fifth day, we were all aware of *only* one Earth." Another astronaut, American Rusty Schweigert, who walked on the moon, had this to say: "From the moon, earth is so small and so fragile and such a precious little spot in the universe that you can block it out with your thumb. Then you realize that on that spot, that beautiful warm blue and white circle, is everything that means anything to you — all of nature and history, music, poetry and art, birth and love and death, tears, joy, prayer, dancing — all of it right there in that little spot that you can cover with your thumb. And then you are changed forever. Your relationship to the world is no longer what it was."[1]

In truth, these are religious experiences. On the brink of the third millennium, a new awareness of planet Earth as one community of life is growing among peoples everywhere. But this appreciation is marked by strong paradox: the more we discern how precious all life on Earth is, the more we also realize alarmingly how human actions are ravaging and exhausting the natural world. Thus the spiritual/ethical question of our right relation with Earth emerges as a new, vitally important issue, one that encompasses all others, including relationship with God and peaceful justice among humans.

never come back again. We are killing birth itself, wiping out the future of our fellow creatures who took millions of years to evolve. We live in a time of a great dying off.

On the one hand, we gaze in wonder at the world; on the other hand, we are wasting the world. These are signs of our Earth's times and should be filled with meaning for people of faith. But the odd thing is that, with some notable exceptions, many religious people and the church as a whole are curiously silent about the Earth. We are like the disciples asleep in the garden of Gethsemane while Earth undergoes its passion and death.

Responses in the Spirit

In spiritual terms, what this time calls for is nothing less than a conversion of our minds and hearts to the good of the Earth. Catholic Christians need to unlearn the dualism that led us to pit the spirit against matter and caused us to pursue paths of holiness marked "flee the world." We need to learn to relate anew to the natural world not as dominators, not even as stewards — which does not go far enough — but as real kin in the one creation of God. Our human lives are interwoven with millions of other species in a great community of life. How we pray and live responsibly in this community will determine whether life on this planet has a glorious or miserable future. The very glory of God is at stake.

There are at least three spiritual responses to Earth's crisis: the sacramental or contemplative, the ascetic, and the prophetic. Each is important; they can be combined in different ways; together they will enable us to develop the virtue of "earthkeeping."[3]

The *sacramental* response gazes contemplatively on the world with the eyes of love rather than with an arrogant, utilitarian stare, and sees there the handiwork of God. Not only is the evolutionary world created by the power and imagination of Holy Wisdom, but it also participates in the goodness of Divine Being. Moreover, in the incarnation God chose to unite with the material of Earth in a profoundly personal way. The resurrection of the crucified Jesus transforms a piece of this Earth, real to the core, into glory in God's eternal presence. This pledges a joyful future beyond death for all people along with the Earth itself, Christ being the firstborn of all creation. Now the humble, earthy materials of bread and wine offer communion in the very body of God.

Seen in this way, the sacramental character of Earth becomes clear. Sacramental theology has always taught that simple material things —

bread, wine, water, oil, the embodied sexual relationship of marriage — can be bearers of divine grace. We now realize that this is
so only because to begin with the Earth with all its creatures is the
original sacrament. "Charged with the glory of God," as poet Gerard Manley Hopkins penned, the world with its beauties and terrors
makes present the loving power of the Creator whose image it reflects.
This response takes delight in the intricate and powerful workings
of nature for their own sake, standing with scientist Louis Agas-
siz, who said, "I spent the summer traveling; I got half-way across
my back yard." At the same time, the eyes of faith appreciate that
the natural world itself is a primary matrix that reveals and makes
God present. Praise and thanks in personal prayer, community liturgy, and church-wide celebrations such as a Creation Sunday are
apt responses.

The *ascetic* response calls for intellectual humility in our assessment
of the human place in the universe and practical discipline in our use
of natural resources. The true purpose of asceticism has always been
to make us fully alive to the movement of grace in our lives and the
movement of the Spirit in the world. It does so by removing what
blocks our sensitivity to divine power and presence. An ecological
asceticism works to restore right relations between humankind and
otherkind distorted by hubris and greed.

Rather than the medieval construct of the hierarchy of being and
honor ascending from the pebble to the peach to the poodle to the
person, all under the sway of the monarchical God at the apex, asceticism reconfigures that pyramid into a circle of life with human beings
thoroughly interwoven with all other creatures, special in virtue of being conscious and free but utterly interdependent on others for their
life. This new paradigm that defines human beings as members of
Earth's community sets off an earthquake in traditional theological
anthropology that overprivileged humans. When coupled with a theology of the all-pervading Creator Spirit of God who does not rule in
a patriarchal way but vivifies and lures, this view charts a path down
from our selfish pedestal toward partnership with Earth's God-given
power of life.

There are also new ways to engage in traditional practices of
fasting, retreats, sojourns in the wilderness, almsgiving, and use of
material things that honor their ecological reality. We do these things
not to make ourselves suffer and not because we're anti-body, but to
become alert to how enslaved we are by the marketplace and its pro-
motion of greed. Our economy is structured to make us overconsume,
with dire effects upon the Earth. This is such a deep structural power

that we are barely conscious of it — as if it were one of the principalities and powers ruling the world. An "Earth-sensuous asceticism"
that is part of an "Earth-affirming spirituality" is one response that
sets us on the path of virtue. The religious vow of poverty itself is
refreshed in this light.

The *prophetic* response moves us to action on behalf of justice
for the Earth. A moral universe limited to the human community
no longer serves the future of life. If the Earth is indeed creation, a
sacrament of the glory of God with its own intrinsic value, then for
Christians, ongoing destruction of Earth bears the marks of deep sin-
fulness. Its bringing violent disfigurement and ongoing death evokes
the prophetic response, with its ethical demands for care, protection,
and restoration. Indeed, the impulse to care for the Earth, to heal and
redeem it, takes on the character of a moral imperative. One stringent
criterion must now measure the morality of our actions: whether or
not these contribute to a sustainable Earth community.

Undergirding this ethic is a startling idea: we need to extend vigor-
ous moral consideration to the nonhuman community of Earth. We
need to respect life and resist the culture of death not only among
humankind but also among other living creatures. In such ethical reflection, the great commandment to love your neighbor as yourself
is extended to include all members of the community. "Who is my
neighbor?" asks Brian Patrick. He answers, "The Samaritan? The
outcast? The enemy? Yes, yes, of course. But it is also the whale, the
dolphin, and the rain forest. Our neighbor is the entire community of
life, the entire universe. We must love it all as our very self." All of
the lessons that Christianity teaches about concern for the poor and
oppressed now become inclusive of the natural world. The common
good now includes the Earth and all living creatures in addition to
humans. We need to repent of our ill treatment of nonhumans. If nature is the new poor, then we must extend the preferential option for
the poor to other species. We must widen compassionate solidarity
with victims and action on behalf of justice to include not only suffering human beings but also life systems and other species. "Save the
rain forest" becomes a concrete moral application of the commandment "Thou shalt not kill." The moral goal is to ensure vibrant life
in community for all.

This in turn requires us to realize the deep connections between
social injustice and ecological devastation. Economic poverty coin-
cides with ecological poverty, for as liberation theologies have argued,
the poor suffer disproportionately from environmental destruction.[4]
Examples redound. In developing countries the onset of economic

development for corporate profit brings deforestation, soil erosion, and polluted waters, which in turn lead to the disruption of local cycles of nature and the sustenance economies on which most poor people depend. Sheer human misery results. Again, lack of land reform pushes dispossessed rural peoples to the edges of cultivated land, where in order to stay alive they practice slash-and-burn agriculture, in the process destroying pristine habitat, killing rare animals, and displacing indigenous peoples. To give a North American example, U.S. companies export work to factories across the Mexican border (*maquiladoras*) that cheaply employ thousands of young, rural women to make high quality consumer goods for export, while they live in unhealthy squalor in an environment spoiled by toxic waste. Ecofeminist theology is replete with other examples of how "the rape of the Earth" and the violation of women's bodies are connected as expressions of patriarchal domination of the life-givers.[5]

In a global perspective, these conditions result from an international economic system driven by profit. Its inner logic makes it prey without ceasing on nature's resources and seek cheap labor to turn these resources into consumer products. And in wealthy countries, too, ecological injustice runs through the social fabric. The economically well-off can choose to live amid acres of green while poor people are housed near factories, refineries, or waste-processing plants that heavily pollute the environment. Birth defects, general ill health, and disease result. The bitterness of this situation is exacerbated by racial prejudice, as environmental racism pressures people of color to dwell in these neighborhoods.

In sum, social injustice has an ecological face. Ravaging of people and of the land go hand in hand. To be truly effective, therefore, prophetic action must not pit issues of social justice against issues of ecological health, but must include commitment to ecological wholeness within the struggle for a more just social order. We all share the status of creature; we are all kin in the evolving community of life now under siege; our vision of justice must be one of cosmic justice. The aim is to establish and protect healthy ecosystems where all living creatures can flourish.

Conclusion

A flourishing humanity on a thriving Earth in an evolving universe, all together filled with the glory of God — such is the theological vision and praxis we are being called to in this critical age of Earth's distress. We need to appreciate all over again that Earth is a sacrament, vivified by the living Spirit of God. We need to realize that the way we are destroying it is tantamount to a sacrilege. And we need to act as members of the Earth community called to be partners with God in the ongoing creation rather than destruction of the world. This moment of crisis calls for a spirituality and ethics that will empower us to live in the web of life as sustainers rather than destroyers of the world. Ignoring this view keeps the church and its members locked into fatal irrelevance while the great drama is being played out in the actual wider world. But being converted to the Earth sets us who are the church and our ministries off on a great spiritual, intellectual, and moral adventure. Instead of living as thoughtless or greedy exploiters, we, by conversion to the Earth, are empowered to rediscover our kinship and live as sisters and brothers, friends and lovers, mothers and fathers, priests and prophets, co-creators and children of the Earth as God's good creation gives us life. This is our generation's great religious adventure, which is absolutely a matter of life or death. No more monumental challenge faces those who are led by the Spirit of God at the start of the third millennium.

Notes

1. See Michael Dowd, *Earthspirit: A Handbook for Nurturing an Ecological Christianity* (Mystic, Conn.: Twenty-Third Publications, 1991), for these Earth quotations.

2. Sallie McFague, *The Body of God: An Ecological Theology* (Minneapolis: Fortress Press, 1993).

3. Larry Rasmussen, *Earth Community, Earth Ethics* (Maryknoll, N.Y.: Orbis Books, 1996). This book is filled with insight taken from church experience.

4. See David Hallman, ed., *Ecotheology: Voices from South and North* (Geneva: WCC Publications; Maryknoll, N.Y.: Orbis Books, 1994); Leonardo Boff and Virgil Elizondo, eds., *Ecology and Poverty* (Maryknoll, N.Y.: Orbis Books, 1995).

5. See Rosemary Radford Ruether, *Gaia and God: An Ecofeminist Theology of Earth Healing* (San Francisco: HarperSanFrancisco, 1992); Elizabeth Johnson, *Women, Earth, and Creator Spirit* (New York: Paulist Press, 1993).

20

World Apartheid

Our Greatest Structural Evil

Tissa Balasuriya, OMI

I am happy to present this article for the *Festschrift* in honor of Sr. Joan D. Chittister, who has been thoughtful and courageous in her writings and actions, inspired by a deep spirituality of loving service to humanity. The spiritual quest is the search for self-realization of the noblest aspirations, for happiness, holiness, and perfection in union with others and the Transcendent, as possible in this life. It engages a person and a community to overcome selfishness, to care for others and share with others what each has, and thus increase the genuine happiness and fulfillment of all.

A materialist approach would make happiness consist in the care-free possession and use of material things by individuals or communities. This can cause unconcern for others, competition, conflicts, wars, and unhappiness even among the affluent.

The core values of the world religions and of secular humanism teach deep concern for the other, respect for life, for truth, justice, sharing, peace, and care of nature, as well as the common good of humanity. These values are quite contrary to those of the prevailing dominant world order, which glorifies wealth and private profit acquired selfishly. In the actual world, inequalities are growing, and have been so during many centuries.

Apartheid is a system or social order in which there is an imposition of superiority of one group over others, as of the white race over the blacks in South Africa. There was almost universal disapproval of the South African policy of apartheid — segregation of the races. But few stop to think that the whole world system is based on a worse form of global apartheid.

From 1492 until the 1950s the colonial empires provided European peoples with living space, lands for plantations, cheap labor, slaves, cheap raw materials, and markets for their products. The powerful European peoples put in place economic, political, social, cultural, and religious structures, relationships, and values to suit their domination over the rest of the world for centuries. Neither the decolonization of the postwar era nor the collapse of the Soviet Union has changed the distribution of land among the world's racial groupings. In 2000 the map of the world, according to racial distribution of population to land, remains more or less the same as in 1900. The present growth of capitalist globalization is very much the worsened continuation of the economic and sociocultural order built up by that earlier global transformation under Western military colonial domination. This "global apartheid" is one of our biggest structural evils.

When the European population was increasing rapidly between 1500 and 1900, it forcibly appropriated most of the vast open spaces of the earth assuming that "might is right." The present frontiers of many nations are basically the result of such European expansion and policies. The different racial groupings remain or are kept in separate "preserves." The yellow peoples have China, Japan, and the adjacent lands. The blacks have Africa. The brown peoples are allotted South and Southeast Asia. The Arabs have North Africa and the Middle East. The rest of the world — Europe, including Russia; North, Central, and South America; Australia; New Zealand — has been largely reserved for the whites.

This is what passes for the present world order, legitimized by the UN system, set up with these national borders as inviolable. It consolidates centuries of European victories, pillage, colonization, exploitation, and marginalization of other peoples. The structural adjustment policies of the IMF and the World Bank do not call for structural improvements in relation to population and land. Only factors such as capital, resources, and technology are considered mobile in the so-called free market and free world. The present distribution of land among the races is taken as an unchangeable absolute.

This basic inequality is a source of other inequalities such as wealth, income, and resources. It deprives needy people in Asia, for example, of land, opportunities for work, food, and a decent livelihood. It leads to an enormous misuse and abuse of land in a world of hunger. It is maintained by unjust migration laws, leading to "illegal" immigration and conflicts. It is a perennial form of injustice for which no solution is in sight due to the present global power syndrome. It so conditions both males and females (mainly Westerners) that there is little questioning of its injustice and of the way it arose. Consequently, the transnational corporations still take over lands and resources of the poor peoples for the benefit, mainly, of the rich in the rich countries.

The tendency to view history from the Western point of view is one factor in the cultural impact of power. Language itself communicates this value pattern. The technologically advanced nations are considered "civilized." Their economic system is supposed to bring about "fair play" through "free markets." Their political forms are regarded as the highest such achievement of humanity. Their military exploits are extolled as extending the frontiers of human progress. Christianity, their nominal religion, is proposed as the salvific communion with the divine.

Western peoples have undoubtedly contributed to the advancement of humanity in the past five centuries. History has records of other expansions of peoples before that. But the European expansion since 1492 is the most impactful change in the map of the world and still determines the present world system. The cultural conditioning within this system is so strong that most universities and educational systems, and even international lawyers, ethicists, and moral theologians, hardly evaluate justly the demands that world justice places upon the imbalance of land distribution.

The foreign debt of poor countries continues the earlier phenomenon of the transfer of resources from the poor to the rich countries. On the other hand, the real debt of the rich former colonial powers to the colonized countries is several times more than the present debt of the poor countries to the rich ones.

This imbalance of land to population is one of the most pernicious obstacles to human development and justice in the distribution of the world's resources. The relatively underpopulated countries — such as the U.S.A., Canada, Brazil, Argentina, Russia, Australia, and New Zealand — have immigration laws that discriminate against Asians and Africans. Those born of white parents have almost the entire underinhabited world open to them in which to settle and reproduce their kind.

Inequities in the relationships of population to land will worsen in the coming decades because the aging populations of the affluent countries are not growing as rapidly as they are in the countries of Asia, Africa, and Latin America. The world will not be able to neglect this problem for long. Peoples without land and food are likely to reach out toward uninhabited or sparsely inhabited lands. This has been the broad historical trend over the centuries. In this perspective the rhetoric of world justice, human rights, peace, debt payment, and aid has to be rethought. There has to be a deconstruction of the dialogue on international law and justice. The just interests of the powerless poor are not taken into account in the discussion of the rich at the summit conferences of the G8. It is not highlighted even in the discourse among the governments of the poor peoples as in the Non-Aligned Movement. There is no rationally planned and just mobility of people to the free and unused lands of the world.

The present world system does not recognize the universal human right to the means of livelihood and hence a just distribution of the Earth space among all humans. It negates God's desire to make the whole Earth available to all humankind. It is basically contrary to the teachings of the world faiths, including those of Jesus, who enjoins the love of God and neighbor as the essential commandment of his gospel: "I was hungry and you gave me to eat.... I tell you this: anything you did here for one of my brothers and sisters, however humble, you did for me" (Matt. 25:35, 40).

God in Jesus identifies with the other, especially the one in need. The fathers of the early church, such as Ambrose of Milan, John Chrysostom, Basil the Great, and Augustine, teach that the goods of the earth belong to all humanity. Therefore, no one should waste what belongs to God and to all, nor accumulate too much to the detriment of the needs of others. This is theft. Unfortunately, the Christian churches have sanctioned and encouraged in various ways the European colonial expansion of the fifteenth century onward. The papal bulls of the fifteenth and sixteenth centuries would have confirmed Christians in these perceptions. For example, Pope Nicholas V stated,

> We, strengthened by Divine love, moved by Christian charity, and bound by the demands of our pastoral office, are desirous, as is fitting, both to encourage what pertains to the integrity and increase of the Faith, for which Christ, our God, shed his blood; and to sustain, in this most holy enterprise, the vigour of souls of those faithful to us and to your Royal Majesty. Therefore by apostolic authority, by the tenor of this letter, we grant to you —

> the full and free faculty to capture and subjugate Saracens and pagans, and other unbelievers and enemies of Christ whomsoever and wheresoever settled;

> to invade and conquer their kingdom, dukedoms, countries, principalities; and other dominions, lands, places, villages, camps, possessions;

to seize any goods whatsoever, whether movable or immovable, which are held and possessed by these same Saracens, pagans, unbelievers, and enemies of Christ;

to reduce to slavery their inhabitants;

to appropriate perpetually for yourselves and your successors, the kings of Portugal, the kingdoms, dukedoms, countries, principalities and other dominions, possessions, and goods of this sort converting them to your own use and utility and that of your successors.

This and similar papal bulls indicate both the dominant theology of the times and the nature of the alliance between the papacy and the kings of Portugal. The spirituality in those times was compatible with such conquests, robbery, and enslavement of peoples. Regrettably, such a theology and spirituality was at least implicitly dominant in the church for several centuries. It was the background thinking in the formation of priests, religious, and laity, even when they were urged to be charitable toward the neighbor. Pastoral practice evolved with this perception of the church's unique salvific mission.

In summary, the land distribution among the racial groups of the world is the greatest structural evil today because it

- is most cruel in its causes and has had a very long-term impact

- is most deeply entrenched as unquestionable in peoples' minds

- has benefited "Christian" peoples and distorted their vision

- has the worst consequences on the lives of poorer peoples

- has a continuing impact of increasing inequities and poverty

- causes (unconscious) corruption of the most developed peoples

- vitiates a valuable UNO system and understanding of human rights

- is most difficult to resolve rationally and peacefully

- is not within the purview of an international court of justice

- will be a cause of future disasters, including conflicts.

Christian theology, spirituality, and action need to be renewed to be just and life-giving to humanity in this gloomy situation. Christian reflection has to help identify the real evils in social, economic, cultural, and political global realities and motivate persons to struggle to reform them. But this struggle brings about personal suffering in sacrificing luxuries for the common good and in facing the determined opposition of the organized forces of social injustice, often consciously or unconsciously backed by the religious establishments. If we take such steps, we will come under attack from the powers that be, and, as was Jesus, we will be crucified.

Facing the evil of global apartheid, peoples of goodwill, including Christians, must opt for alternative models of human relations and alternative paths to global transformation based on the values of freedom, justice, sharing, truth, peace, and planned adjustment of land and resources to meet peoples' needs. Consequently, a just world order would be one in which

1. every human person is respected as a person, without discrimination, and is insured the basic essentials of life;

2. each community is able to provide the basic amenities for the good life and cultural development of its members;

3. the planet Earth is cared for to be a suitable home for present and future humanity.

For these to be realized, a world authority should be empowered to bring about a planned and peaceful reallocation of land to peoples. It is one way in which the differential growth of peoples can be creatively related to the occupation and use of the earth. It need not increase pollution and waste, since poor peoples, unlike the present affluent occupants of North America and Australia, have long traditions of earth care.

European expansionism from 1500 to 1950 need not set the pattern of land distribution for humanity's long-term future. The main orientation of global land policy should be that, with existing populations insured their due rights, persons without land should have planned access to land without persons. There should be settlement policies and programs for moving needy, land-hungry people to scantily populated areas such as Canada, Australia, the western part of the United States, and areas of Latin America — in addition to migration within existing national borders. The words "developed" and "underdeveloped," used in terms of technological advance, could also be understood in relation to the number of persons supported by a landmass. Thus, for example, Bangladesh, with 55,000 square miles, supports 128 million persons, whereas New Zealand supports only 3.8 million on 104,000 square miles. Which land is more developed?

Population resettlement is one way of compensating for the past injustice of plundering the resources of poor peoples by colonization and for the present inequities in international economy. It could profitably use lands presently uncultivated to help reduce malnutrition, which now affects over five hundred million persons. This would increase employment in the land-rich countries also. Is not large-scale unemployment in the U.S.A., Canada, and Australia due not so much to overpopulation as to underpopulation and a poor use of resources? More inhabitants would mean more demand, more employment, and more dynamism, as shown by the economy of the United States, which has grown much faster than that of Canada, though both were settled by whites at about the same time. Further, a more open policy on resettling immigrants would reduce billions of dollars spent on armaments.

Planned resettlement of millions of persons per year in the underdeveloped areas of the world is a feasible proposal today if there is the political will to carry it out. Hundred of millions cross national frontiers and the oceans each year as tourists. World refugees number tens of millions. It would not mean reducing Australia, Canada, or the U.S.A. in size, but increasing the number of North Americans and Australians at a much faster rate than at present. This would then increase the national wealth of land-rich countries such as Argentina, Bolivia, and Brazil. However, all manner of arguments are alleged — from cultural differences to the lifeboat theory of triage and survival of the fittest — for not considering such alternatives.

Because culture is a real problem, the process of the reallocation of lands and populations would have to include other imaginative creative provisions — for example, that western Canadians be settled in the western part of U.S.A. Then the area from Alaska to Vancouver and east to Winnipeg could absorb several tens of millions of Chinese who would doubtless make better use of the land. Fair provision would have to be made for the Amerindians in those regions. The world order of national frontiers that decided to suit white people is inadequate to meet the challenges of today and tomorrow. Human beings and human right to life are more important than arbitrarily created national boundaries. All these are far less costly and far more profitable than space travel, arms production, or even the amount spent by the affluent on pet foods.

We are all called to transcend our narrow particularities in order to arrive at a higher, wider, and deeper level of sharing among all human beings. This demands an inner transformation of ourselves to accept all others as sisters and brothers. Our growth to a planetary dimension is an invitation to spiritual deepening, a purification from selfishness to a more universal communion in real life, to our own humanization. Insofar as we do so, we shall become more truly civilized, approach the ideals of the best in all our religions and cultures, and pursue the deepest aspirations of every human heart and mind. This world crisis summons us to evolve a new type of human person, conscious of better values, relationships, and structures.

For such changes to occur leadership has to be spirit-inspired, nonviolent, and based on networking locally, regionally, and globally. The leadership of credible service and personal sacrifice as shown in the lives of Mahatma Gandhi, Martin Luther King Jr., and Nelson Mandela can help overcome this global apartheid without violence among peoples. The world of the twenty-first century will not be circumscribed within the framework of the nineteenth century and of 1945. We need the vision and courage to dare turn back the processes of history — perhaps an impossible dream. But the forced structures of yesterday are not adequate for the problems of tomorrow.

21

Finding the Face of God in an Age of Globalization

Patricia M. Mische

What is the most important spiritual question of our time? My quick response to such a big, wide-open question settles on big, wide-open words — words like *life* and *death, the holy* or *sacred, ultimacy, meaning, identity, belonging, communion, community, unity, diversity, justice* and *peace, suffering, order (cosmos)* and *disorder (chaos), morality* and *ethics, creation* and *creativity, faith, hope,* and *love.*

Questions related to all these words and concepts have been spiritually important in all ages, from the beginnings of human consciousness and the human spiritual journey. But in each period of human history a prior question must be asked: What time is it now? What is the historical context in which these concerns and questions at the core of spiritual and religious development are being explored, experienced, interpreted, and expressed? How and to what extent are they shaping souls and civilizations and affecting the evolution of the planet and community of life?

What time is it now in the history of the human community and the evolution of the planet? When looked at from economic, historical, political, military, cultural, communications, and environmental perspectives, this is clearly a period of intense globalization. But this outer, material globalization has not yet been matched by a commensurate spiritual globalization. While much progress has been made in interreligious dialogue and a resurgence of spirituality of many varieties inside and outside traditional religious traditions, and by movements for global ethics that include religious and secular thinkers alike, these movements have not grown in pace with forces of economic, military, and other material forms of globalization.

Material Growth

The twentieth century was marked by exponential growth. Human populations multiplied at least four times, from 1.6 billion in 1900 to 6 billion in 1999. In the millions of years of human existence that preceded the year 1850, the total human population at any one time had never exceeded one billion. By the middle of the twenty-first century, human populations are expected to double again to more than ten billion.[1] Ninety percent of this ten billion will be in African, Asian, and Latin American countries, doubling current populations in these regions. According to some estimates the Earth cannot support more than 2.5 billion people at the economic level now enjoyed by the twenty-four most developed countries, yet most of the world's people aspire to this standard of living.

In that same twentieth century, the global economy multiplied enormously from an annual output of $2.3 trillion in 1900 to $39 trillion in 1998. The growth in economic output for just three years, from 1995 to 1998, exceeded that during the ten thousand years from the beginning of agriculture until 1900.[2] Per capita income multiplied more than four times, from $1,500 to $6,600, with most of this increase coming in the second half of the century. The life expectancy average increased from thirty-five years in 1900 to sixty-six years in 1999. More food was produced in the twentieth century than ever before, and human products poured into the global market place — and into the Earth's biosphere — at a record rate.

In one sense these figures represent tremendous human success. Advancements in science, medicine, industry, and technology made it possible for more people to live longer, healthier, and more productive lives. But these figures also portend serious problems to come in the twenty-first century. The benefits of this growth were not evenly distributed. Most of the benefits are going to one-fifth of the world population who live better lives than ever before, while another one-fifth at the bottom struggle to survive with no or little access to safe water, or adequate nutrition, shelter, education, and employment.

Moreover, the costs of human growth to the larger Earth community have not yet been calculated. In the twentieth century the world lost close to 50 percent of its original forest area. This in turn caused increased flooding, soil erosion, the depletion of aquifers, and a diminished capacity to absorb carbon emissions that cause global warming. A fivefold increase in fossil fuel use since the 1980s contributed to atmospheric concentrations of CO_2 that are at the highest level in 150,000 years and are beyond the capacity of nature to absorb. As a consequence, world temperatures are rising. The thirteen warmest years since records began to be kept in 1866 all occurred in the 1980s and 1990s. Severe heat threatens food productivity and human life.[3]

Whereas soil formation exceeded soil erosion throughout most of the Earth's evolution, in this century a combination of overplowing, overgrazing, and deforestation reversed the relationship. We have crossed a threshold of unsustainability. Each year the Earth community loses millions of tons of topsoil, depleting the Earth's fertility and undermining its food-producing capacities.[4]

The twentieth century also saw more pollutants and toxic chemicals dumped into air, soil, and water than in all previous centuries. Radioactive emissions from nuclear weapons production, testing, and stockpiling entered the air, soil, water, and ultimately the DNA and human gene pool, affecting the viability of future generations.

This presents a tremendous moral challenge for today's generation. We are stealing from our children and grandchildren. Moreover, we are undermining their very capacity to be born and to live in health. Children are more vulnerable than adults to pollutants, and unborn children are the most vulnerable of all, especially in the embryonic stage, when organs begin to form. The right to a healthy environment may be the ultimate right-to-life issue. Birth defects, learning disabilities, cancers, and chronic illnesses appear to be rising among children. In the latter half of the twentieth century more and more chemicals were added to the environment that could cause birth defects and damage the reproductive organs of men and women.[5]

Future generations are also threatened by the emissions of chlorofluorocarbons and other ozone-depleting gases that are producing a hole in the Earth's ozone layer, exposing people and the Earth community to higher amounts of the sun's ultraviolet rays. Those yet to come will pay the greatest price in the form of increased cancers, diminished food supplies, and other ill effects.

We have new powers over life and death never dreamed of by our ancestors — powers that in the past were ascribed only to God. We can develop new species in test tubes and clone existing ones. We can also cause the elimination of millions of plant and animal species that evolved through eons of natural selection. In the twentieth century humans caused a wave of mass species extinctions that was unequaled in all previous centuries of human history combined. It has been calculated that in the three centuries between 1600 and 1900 humans accounted for the loss of one species every four years. After 1900 the rate began increasing to one per year, and by 1979 to one a day. Depending on whose calculations are used, by 1999 the estimated losses were between one and twenty-seven thousand species a year.[6] This magnitude of loss has occurred only five times before in 1.5 billion years of life on Earth — all of those from natural causes. The greatest was the Permian extinction 245 million years ago, when 95 percent of all known animal species were lost. The most recent was the Cretaceous extinction sixty-five million years ago, when 76 percent of all species were lost, including the dinosaurs, possibly due to a meteorite hitting the Earth. It took millions of years following each of these extinctions for the Earth to recover its previous level of biodiversity.

The mass extinctions now underway are caused by humans and could be avoided through a change in consciousness and human choices of behavior. If we fail to learn lessons and make necessary changes in our behavior, we may be on our way to losing two-thirds of all living species. The species themselves will be gone forever. Not even God will be able to bring them back, because the conditions in which they were first created will have changed. And it will take the Earth millions of years to recover the level of biodiversity it had in 1900. Unless we change our consciousness and behavior, future generations of humans will live on a planet of weeds, for only weedy creatures are likely to survive today's mass extinction. Here, "weedy" means creatures that reproduce quickly, spread rapidly, and survive almost anywhere — rats, cockroaches, pigeons, feral dogs, sparrows, crows, and humans. These will be left to cohabit the Earth.[7]

Forests — especially tropical forests — are critically linked to Earth's biodiversity. According to FAO, the rate of deforestation in tropical countries has increased since the 1970s to a loss of 15.4 million hectares (38.5 million acres) per year, with South America losing 6.2 million hectares per year, Southeast Asia 1.6 percent of its forests. The Philippines, once nearly covered with forests, has lost 92 percent. By the middle of the next century tropical rainforests will exist virtually nowhere outside protected areas. These "protected" areas, which now encompass 6.3 percent of the planet's land area, do not retain their full biological diversity.

The question before us is not whether the Earth will survive human assaults, for the Earth, as it has through its long evolution, will adapt in some way and continue to evolve. The question is whether humans will be able to survive the adaptations that the Earth makes in response to human assaults, and if so, what it will mean to be human. Human cultures and spirituality are greatly shaped by the natural environment. As Thomas Berry has pointed out, if we lived in a place devoid of other life, like the moon, we would be very different beings. Future generations growing up on an Earth that has lost its biodiversity may be impoverished in mind and spirit.

Globalization and Interdependence

Increasing globalization makes these threats even more complex. We are in a new historical situation in which human decisions and activities in one region dramatically affect the ecological and economic well-being of the entire Earth community. National and local communities have increasingly been penetrated by global economic forces beyond their control. Instead of democratic governance of, by, and for the people, governance is increasingly being ceded to global market forces. Foreign direct investments have more than tripled from the mid-1980s to the mid-1990s. And the power and wealth of some transnational corporations now exceed those of many nation-states. Fifty-one of the world's hundred largest economies are now economies internal to corporations. About 29 percent of economic activity worldwide is generated by only two hundred corporations that are linked by strategic alliances and interlocking boards.[8]

Rich and poor countries alike are confronted by the need to survive growing global competition for favorable balances of trade and payments, and for access to scarce resources, markets, and new technologies. The drive for economic security and a competitive edge in the world market has led many countries to subordinate long-term ecological concerns to short-term economic goals.

All countries face this dilemma. But the poorest countries, especially those that have borrowed heavily from international banks and agencies to finance economic development programs, are especially pressured. Faced by debilitating foreign debts, rising interest rates, adverse terms of trade, interrupted financial flows, and conditionalities imposed by lending agencies, many have resorted to overusing their resource base, exporting precious natural resources (their ecological capital) and ignoring environmental degradation. Worse, many poor countries have become the dumping ground for toxic waste from the richer countries. With tougher environmental protection laws at home, many industries in the rich countries now do the most polluting aspects of their production in poor countries, where standards are weak or not enforced, or illegally dump toxic waste in poor countries.

Environmental degradation and resource scarcity have already contributed to conflicts, civil strife, and warfare in many world regions in past history and contemporary times. These include Somalia, the Sudan, and Ethiopia in the Horn of Africa; the Middle East, where water and oil are critical; the Philippines, Papua New Guinea, Haiti, Honduras, El Salvador, and more. In the twenty-first century, with growing populations competing for increasingly scarce resources, we can expect even more conflict and warfare related to vital resources. Environmental sustainability and more equitable economic distribution are thus essential to global peace and security in the twenty-first century.[9]

Today, the people of all countries are inextricably bound together in one interdependent Earth community. The bottom line for economic security is ecological sustainability. At the same time, the path to ecological integrity is linked to resolving global economic problems, especially gross inequities. Such prospects require a major transformation in the way we think about our relationship to the Creator, the Earth, and one another.

What kind of Earth, what kind of humanity, what kind of human spirit are we developing for ourselves and future generations? In the past, when groups exceeded the limits of environmental sustainability, they moved on to new territorial frontiers. But now there are few, if any, new territorial frontiers, and many countries are loath to absorb more refugees into already oversized populations. But the habit of looking to a new frontier to resolve economic and environmental limits is deeply imbedded. In the absence of new territorial frontiers, some look for new technological frontiers to fix the problem. But while appropriate technology may help resolve some environmental problems, it cannot resolve them all. A danger is that people addicted to overconsumption and environmentally destructive habits, and those that aspire to such consumption, will blindly place their trust in a technological fix in order to avoid making fundamental changes in their patterns of behavior and relationship with the Earth community.

A Global Spirituality

The most important new frontier for redressing these issues and healing the Earth community now is that of mind and spirit. We need to take responsibility for the state of our soul and the state of our world. The new web of global interdependencies that bind us together, and the tremendous stresses and complex moral choices before us in the twenty-first century, require a far deeper and more far-reaching spirituality than ever before in history.

True spirituality can never be an escape from life's problems. God, the sacred center at the source of all authentic spiritual journeys, must be met in the midst of life, not in escape from life. Today, we live in a global age — an age of planetary exploration and communications and global interdependence. Our spiritual journey — the quest for life in God — must be undertaken now in a global as well as local context, as responsible members of a global community. Our spirituality must be a global spirituality. Without a strong spirituality, including awareness of divine love and creativity at work in the world, people are not motivated, empowered, or sustained in work for the global common good.

A New Global Order

The twenty-first century faces tremendous problems and tremendous promise. Old orders and systems are dying, inadequate to respond effectively to the new dangers and opportunities of an interdependent world. A "new world order" has not yet been born.

The birthing needed is not of a new world order only slightly modified from the bipolar era of standoffs between the U.S. and the U.S.S.R. Nor is it the "new" version built around U.S. military domination or G8 economic domination. The new world order called for must be based on deep awareness of our kinship and common dependency on the Earth and one another, and on deepened commitment to values of peace, social justice, economic well-being, respect for cultural diversity, and the integrity of creation, with the democratic participation of all the world's peoples.

Such a truly new world order needs to be born within us first, in a transformed consciousness, in a right ordering of our spirit, mind, heart, and will. Real changes, the real transformations in history, have begun with inner spiritual changes. This new order must also be born in the outer order of the world community in the form of new systems of greater justice and peace in a right ordering of our international relationships and structures. A new ordering of the soul requires and seeks a new ordering of the larger world, an ordering rooted in wisdom and compassion.

Thus, to answer "What is the most important spiritual question of our time?" we return to where we began. The key concepts are now, as always, life and death; unity and diversity; meaning and ultimacy; consciousness and oneness with the sacred and holy; justice and peace; good and evil; faith, hope, and love; imagination and creativity to overcome adversity; belonging and community. But these core concepts have to be understood anew, and find meaning and expression, in a new global context. We live in a time of increasing global interdependence and a struggle to learn to live together in a global community. And the face of God in this time will be discovered to be a God of interdependence and global community.

Notes

1. Lester R. Brown and Christopher Flavin, "A New Economy for a New Century," in *State of the World, 1999,* ed. Linda Starke (New York: W. W. Norton, 1999), 8.

2. Ibid., 10.

3. Lester R. Brown, "The Future of Growth," in *State of the World, 1998,* ed. Linda Starke (New York: W. W. Norton, 1998), 10.

4. Ibid., 8–9.

5. See Lloyd Timberlake and Laura Thomas, *When the Bough Breaks: Our Children, Our Environment* (London: Earthscan Publications, 1990).

6. John Tuxill, "Appreciating the Benefits of Plant Biodiversity," in *State of the World, 1999,* uses the figure of one thousand per year. Norman Myers, in his speech at Eco Ed, an international conference on environment and development held in Toronto in October 1992, estimated twenty-seven thousand a year.

7. David Quammen, "Planet of Weeds: Tallying the Losses of Earth's Animals and Plants," *Harpers Magazine* (October 1999): 57–69.

8. Bread for the World, *Hunger in a Global Economy* (Washington, D.C.: Bread for the World, 1998).

9. For a fuller treatment of relationships between environmental degradation and civil strife and war, see Patricia M. Mische, "Ecological Security in a New World Order: Some Linkages between Ecology, Peace and Global Security," in *Non-Military Aspects of International Security* (Paris: UNESCO, 1995).

22

Biophilia or Necrophilia?

The Most Important Spiritual Question of Our Time

Matthew Fox

Clearly, there are so many important spiritual questions in our time. Here are some for starters: What is the relationship of mysticism to prophecy, of love to spiritual warriorhood, of experience of the Divine to the struggle for justice, of humans to the rest of nature? How do we honor women's wisdom and the wisdom of oppressed peoples, whose voices have been taken away so often and in so many ways by so many forces? Where will we find forms of worship that do justice to our capacity for praise and forms of education that do justice to our capacity for learning? Who will lead us in our efforts to simplify lifestyles and to reinvent work so that it can be a worthy receptacle for the purging and passing on of our values of justice, compassion, and ecojustice? Will we ever be able to enjoy one another's differences and participate fully in the divine imagination, which so amply displays its wonderful diversity by sharing multiple colors, kinds, and shades of differences? How will we arrive at a new relating of our spiritual (as distinct from merely religious) traditions so that as a species we may bring forth *all* our shared wisdom at this time when we must move from knowledge to wisdom in order to survive?

All this poses the following: "What one question is the most important question?" To respond, I wish to attempt to narrow these questions down to one or maybe the "question behind the questions."

I see *creation and our attitude toward it* as being the issue behind the issues. It is our lack of trust of nature — our own and others' — that seems to lie behind so many of the mistaken paths that humans take to protect themselves from one another and from nature itself. It is lack of trust in creation that forces humans to play god and to ignore the gift of existence itself, preferring control to letting be.

Scholars of the historical Jesus all agree that Jesus was nature based and remarkably unbiblically based in his spirituality. This is typical of the wisdom tradition wherein creation itself is looked to as a source of revelation. Moreover, the earliest texts of Christianity, texts that gave birth ultimately to the Gospels, show a nature-based spiritual awareness among the earliest Christian communities. The Q documents, from the Q community shortly after Jesus' death, offer an "express appeal to nature as a manifestation of the divine," according to Q scholar Burton L. Mack in his book *The Lost Gospel*.[1]

Also, in the earliest Q document, according to Mack, we see a powerful adaptation of the royal person theme of ancient Israel to a nature-based spirituality. The movement of philosophical wanderers or cynics to which Jesus belonged "used the royal metaphor to advantage. In their case, taking control of one's life required extrication from the social scene. They lived 'according to nature,' they said, and the natural order was imagined as a realm of divine rule in opposition to the prevailing social order."[2] Thus, cosmology offered the basic critique for society and the basic model for ethical living. Kingdom and creation were often identified and so too was the kingdom and the new movement. As Mack argues, "The location of God's kingdom was to be found precisely in the social formation of the movement."[3] The opposite of kingdom was the social order of the day, which was so distant from the kingdom of God, where justice and peace were thought to reign. The Q people believed strongly that "all of nature is God's domain and all kinds of people are under his care."[4] Thus, a clear move beyond tribalism was at hand. The judgment theme came only with Q2, a later version of this document.

Creation is what gets our various religious and spiritual traditions to mix and intermix. It carries us beyond tribalism because no ecosystem or river or ocean or field is labeled Christian or Catholic, Buddhist or Protestant, Baptist or Lutheran. There is an *interbeing* of religion just as there is an interbeing permeating all relationships in the universe, to borrow from Thich Naht Hahn's phrase for our common interconnectivity. Deep ecumenism, the coming together of the world's spiritual traditions around spiritual practice and eco- and social justice, flows from this religious interbeing.

To bring creation and the awe, reverence, wonder, and gratitude it solicits back to the heart of religious and spiritual practice is to bring the Goddess back and to welcome the wisdom of indigenous peoples who never forsook creation in their ritual or prayer or spiritual mindset. It is also to stand up to the seductive myths of consumer society that would substitute anthropocentrism and the purchasing of things for the awe that comes with wonder and living celebratively in a wondrous cosmos. Rabbi Abraham Heschel warned us: "Forfeit your sense of awe and the universe becomes a market place for you." The choice seems to be this: the cosmos as a relationship of awe or the cosmos as a place to buy things.

One reason awe is in short supply in our culture is that more progressively minded religion has so often sold out to the rationalistic ideologies of the modern European era — forces and academic forms that neglect the heart and soul and lower chakras in their pursuit of truth. A living spirituality opts for spirit and heart, body and celebration, grieving and the holy imagination that make all relationships come alive in living rituals. It must divorce itself consciously and deliberately — and this includes, especially, our so-called seminaries or training grounds for spiritual leaders — from an academic system that has sold its soul to forces of rationalism. It must opt for models of learning that include soul, heart, and body, that educate all the chakras, that refuse to perpetuate the rationalism of patriarchal mindsets that have made empire building so successful over the centuries.[5] There must be room for awe and wonder, reverence and radical amazement. There must be room for nothingness and emptiness, for grief and suffering, to be included in our educational forms. There must be room for moral imagination and holy imagination at many levels of self and society. And for mysticism. Only mystics should teach in science labs. Awe and wonder need to return.

One important lesson to learn from creation is its generosity. Creation is generous. Consider this lesson learned from the sun by the medieval Sufi mystic Hafiz.

> Even after all this time
> The sun never says to the earth,
>   "You owe me."
> Look what happens
> with a love like that,
> It lights up the Whole Sky.[6]

Generosity is learned by watching creation. Not only the sun is generous, but parents also are often called upon to be generous. And elders are generous, and lovers and friends are generous. We are a species capable of generosity.[7] Generosity is related etymologically to creation and kinship (Genesis, for example) and creativity (generativity) and givingness. Generosity is like compassion: both are required elements of full living but both seem in rather short supply in our institutions and in our species at this time. We have old lessons to learn from the sun, earth, and sky: how the sun gives so much away and does not ask the earth for repayment. Instead, as Hafiz observes, it lights up the whole sky. Can we learn our capacity for generosity all over again from creation and from the many saints like Gandhi and King and Dorothy Day, who were generous?

Can the Holy Spirit move our species to its next level of evolutionary development — one in which generosity and joy, justice and compassion, reign? That indeed would mean ushering in the kingdom of God. Is this too ambitious an undertaking? Isn't it true that the Spirit that hovered over the waters at the beginning of creation and over the fetal waters of Mary's womb *is* ambitious? Maybe we need to get over our acedia and develop ambitions that take us beyond shopping malls, off the golf courses, and beyond academic infighting to awaken our capacities for compassion and generosity. Maybe we ought to be imitating nature more, finding the divine elements in it, just as the first generation of Christians did, responding to the example and teachings of Jesus.

Creation is not an affectation. It is all that is. It is what we eat, what we see, what we hear, touch, feel, think, dream, *are*. It is our bodies and our souls. Our breath and our feelings, our children and our parents, our ancestors, our DNA and our lineage. It is land, birds, animals, fish, sky, sun, moon, wheat, crops, stars, death, suffering, pain, separation, and much more. All our relations. Yet, we often take creation for granted. Or we participate in destroying it and controlling it rather than honoring it and learning from it.

The question is thus posed: What is the most important spiritual question of our time? I would, in light of my previous reflections, give this answer: Is what we are doing (is what I am doing) contributing to biophilia or to necrophilia? That is the most important question of our time: Are we choosing life over death on a daily basis in all of our activities — work, education, child rearing, retirement, worship — in all our relations? If we are not contributing to love of life (biophilia), then we are probably contributing to love of death (necrophilia). Aquinas says, "God is life, per se life." To contribute to life is to contribute to the God-life. To contribute to death is to contribute to the God-death (crucifixion?). The Wisdom Scriptures say, "This is wisdom: To love life." To choose biophilia is to choose wisdom. The Christ says, "I have come that you may have life and have it in abundance." Abundant biophilia. That is the promise. We do have choices, as individuals and as a species.

The question unfolds in the following manner: What are we doing daily to teach biophilia? (If we are not teaching biophilia, we are contributing to the plethora of necrophiliac lessons being taught regularly in our culture through advertising, omission, bad religion, and toxic professionalism.) We teach biophilia by honoring the body and its inner beauty, by honoring all seven chakras, not just the upper ones, by contributing to making rituals live and come alive, by positions we take against rape of the land and of peoples, by teaching the new cosmology and our sacred origin stories, by learning forms of meditation that tame the reptile brain in us, by learning how to analyze injustice and do something about bringing about justice — in short, by teaching love of life.

Notes

1. Burton L. Mack, *The Lost Gospel: The Book of Q and Christian Origins* (San Francisco: HarperSanFrancisco, 1993), 122.

2. Ibid., 126.

3. Ibid., 127.

4. Ibid., 128.

5. In my book *Sins of the Spirit, Blessings of the Flesh* (New York: Crown, 1999) I treat the chakras in considerable detail and relate them to the seven capital sins of the West, including rationalism, an offense against the sixth chakra.

6. Daniel Lakinsky, trans., *The Gift: Poems by Hafiz the Great Sufi Master* (New York: Penguin/Arkana, 1999), 34.

7. See Fox, *Sins of the Spirit, Blessings of the Flesh,* 332–36.

23

The Dawning of a New Day—
The Telling of a New Story

Elaine M. Wainwright

Everything in the spiritual landscape is becoming permeable and porous once more. Despite all our human engineering and the anthropomorphic checks and balances we reinvent time and time again, God's spirit blows fresh breezes across the barren deserts of sacred traditions and time-honored institutions. A new day is dawning over the spiritual landscape and new possibilities for spiritual pilgrimage open up on all sides.[1]

–DIARMUID O'MURCHU

The closing decades of the twentieth century were characterized by emerging processes or spirit movements that changed the face of the spiritual landscape of the Earth community. As it faces into not only a new century but a new millennium, such a turning toward the new carries both symbolic and actual potential for the dawning of a new day/s. But initially, let's recapitulate. Movements for justice, for liberation, and for peace drew together peoples from a wide range of both human and religious traditions in a work that challenged both the institutions and the narratives of those traditions to their core. The feminist/women's movement raised human consciousness to the inordinate gender disparity in almost all cultures and social systems in today's world, and to the language, narratives, and symbol systems that render women all but invisible. And most recently a growing recognition of the profound significance of the ecological movement called for both a new consciousness and a new way of being in the Earth community.

Each of these movements, as O'Murchu suggests, blew "fresh breezes across the barren deserts of sacred traditions and time-honored institutions." It was as if nothing within the political, social, and cultural/religious worlds was left untouched. As a result, such movements were approached fearfully by some as a time of extraordinary "disintegration," a breaking down of the "time honored" and the "true." They called forth fundamentalist responses that clung, at times fanatically, to a particular institution, belief, or articulation of that belief, regardless of other human and religious values or practices.

For many others, however, these movements were and are seen as movements of the life-spirit, the life-force, the divine spirit that permeates the Earth community and its unfolding. They invited participants into processes of deep reflection and grounded praxis toward human, social, cultural, and cosmic transformation. These movements have only just begun; their inherent processes are in an embryonic stage of evolution. The invitation, the challenge into the twenty-first century and the third millennium, is toward the interrelationship, the spiraling interconnectedness of these processes beyond hierarchal dualisms and binary oppositions: of love and justice, of the material and spiritual, of the ethical and the ritual, of the processes for life and transformation that are emerging in this day. These are the processes that will engage the spiritual quest of those entering a new age of human, of cosmic, unfolding.[2] It is these processes which I will address in the remainder of this essay.

Attentiveness to the spirit, to what is life-enhancing and what is death-dealing in human experience, has been a hallmark of both liberation movements and the emerging theologies closely connected to these movements. This attentiveness has led to a deeper human consciousness and narration of stories of oppression and destruction, not only of the human, but also of the Earth or planetary community, which encompasses all life, all entities, all participants in the entire ecological system. Awareness of and response to the systemic nature of this oppression has, however, sometimes blinded the human community to the interconnectedness of the personal, the interpersonal, the structural, and the ecological, and to the profound relationship between the life-enhancing and the death-dealing, which the natural world demonstrates daily. Attentiveness to the spirit is, therefore, a process which calls forth a new listening within one's own being to the irrevocable interlinking of life and death and to this movement within one's relationships with others and within the universe. Such attentiveness will discern those death-dealing elements which are destructive of life and the life-giving ones which are enhancing of life. From this, new stories of the spirit or life-force at the heart of each relational encounter will emerge, while the shadow of death-dealing will likewise be named with courage and fidelity.

Analysis of these human experiences draws on the human wisdom developed during the twentieth century in the human and social sciences — psychology, sociology, and anthropology. This process discerns and affirms what is indeed the wisdom of the spirit in these disciplines. It then engages this wisdom in a way that enables an uncovering of ideologies, a naming of pathologies, an understanding of human, social, and cultural systems, and a further uncovering of the life-enhancing and the death-dealing. Such analysis brings the processes of the mind or intellect into dialogue with those of the body or the experiential in a way that seeks to be integrative — moving backward and forward and in all manner of directions between and among these processes. It calls for a new wisdom that, like that of the ancient wisdom traditions, draws on life and the knowledge or sciences of life experience as a profound source of the spirit. Thus, the dialogic of human and religious traditions, which has often been isolated into an oppositional dualism, will be reestablished to the enrichment of these traditions and of the life of the Earth community.

Telling the story of the human encounter with the divine or life-enhancing spirit has characterized the spiritual pilgrimage of those within most religious and spiritual traditions. That telling, however, is always a retelling as communities in each new era encounter the divine and the human in new ways. The processes of articulating the human experiences of this era and analyzing them have necessarily led to a profoundly felt need to retell the grand narratives of human and religious history. The awareness that these grand narratives are no longer functioning as they once did has been articulated significantly by postmodernism as one of the ways of naming this present time. What this retelling is calling forth and will continue to call forth is a new imagination together with a new engagement with the spiritual symbols and traditions of this era and with those of myriad other religious and cultural stories within human and planetary history. The emerging narratives will, therefore, be multiple, pluriform, and always in process.

Such a process is already underway, perhaps most explicitly in the feminist and ecofeminist movements. From these movements has emerged a profound consciousness that the very naming of divinity is characterized almost exclusively by patriarchal and power-dominant names, titles, metaphors, and images — king, lord, destroying warrior, father, wronged husband, ultimate authority, avenger, to name but a few. These are woven into the warp and woof of the Jewish and Christian sacred stories and their enactment in ritual and celebration. A variety of sources are, however, nourishing new namings of divinity within the telling of sacred stories. The sacred narrative itself has been plumbed for alternative images and metaphors that draw on female imagery — the womb of God, nursing mother, birth-giver, mother eagle, she-bear, bakerwoman, midwife, Sophia/Wisdom. The bread baked by female hands, the blood and water shed from birth-giving female bodies, inform or reinform the sacred symbol system; each evokes multiple images of divinity, humanity, and their interconnectedness in ways that provide entry into mystery rather than exclusion of so many from that mystery. The long history of female symbolizations of divinity, silenced by the emergence of patriarchal religions, provides a rich source for the new stories. Further, the billions-of-years-long story of the universe and the evocation of imagery from the new science — fractals, strange attractors, and more — also require a new articulation of the story of human and cosmic relationships with divinity.

It is not only images of divinity but of humanity, of all living beings and their interrelationship, that will need new language, that will engage a new imagination, that will find articulation in new stories.[3] In this regard, the sacred stories of indigenous peoples will provide a rich resource — the native Americans of the American continents, aboriginal dreaming in the Australian context, ancient stories from the peoples of Asia, Africa, and the Pacific. These, however, cannot be appropriated into a new colonizing story, but must infuse the spiritual stories of the new dawning of the Earth community with values that have been lost in Western industrialized, capitalist, religious traditioning. Language of interconnectedness and mutual interdependence will replace language of dominance. The voice of every living entity, both human and other than human, will be heard toward the enrichment of the new story, and those voices will be heard according to their own unique contribution to the story of the universe, as well as their resistance to anything that diminishes that contribution.[4]

The new stories will require two accompanying processes if they are to flourish in a way that will transform human consciousness and human activity. First, there must be an engagement of a new ethic, a new way of being in the world, a way that is ancient as well as new. Verses 10 and 11 of Psalm 85, quoted previously in note 2, use the word "righteousness," as do what could justly be called the charter of Christian ethics, the Beatitudes, particularly the fourth and eighth respectively. This righteousness, understood as the right or just ordering of all relationships, is the goal of the movements toward justice and transformation. The difficulty of attaining such righteousness, or right ordering, was emphasized most profoundly for me recently in an address given by bell hooks to an auditorium filled with colleagues who have been working toward this transformative goal for three decades or more. She asked the audience, as it faced a new century and new millennium, At what moment did we cease to infuse our social movements with love?[5] This engagement with a new ethic, a reordering of all relationships within the Earth community so they are relationships of love, will require a most extraordinary attentiveness to the life-force or spirit in our world. This is because the death-dealing powers that work toward the rape and pillaging, consumption and exploitation of the earth, its resources, and its peoples are visibly present, palpably felt, and can engage the human spirit in anger and bitterness.

The human spirit needs a context of ongoing spiritual enrichment in order to remain faithful to this ethic of right relationships. This will be provided in the enactment of new rituals as the context for the retelling of the sacred stories. For so many in today's world, religious ritual has become a familiar but empty combination of movements, words, and symbols that fails to enrich and sustain a life of ethical engagement and spirit attentiveness. Ritualization of the new stories, like their retelling, will not be a rejection of the old but will draw the material symbols of human and religious tradition and of earth sustainability into new meaning — making. Bread and wine, together with earth, air, fire, and water, can be infused with new meaning within the context of a new story. The pouring of water, sprinkling of ashes, burning of incense, and the use of a variety of symbols of materiality in the context of re-membering and re-creating can evoke new levels of consciousness of divine-human-cosmic relationships. Like the images of divinity, they will need to be multiple and varied in response to human need and variety of context. In this way, new stories will find their expression not only in human ethics, but in engaged enactment of their new language and symbols.

The voices, the stories of the Other — other than male, other than Western, other than capitalist, other than white, other than human, and so forth — are emerging toward the dawn of a new era. They are heralding a breaking forth of the spirit of the earth, of the human community, of the divine life-force. Processes are emerging among those who are seeking to be attentive to this spirit, to be engaged in this rebirth. A new listening to experience in the Earth community and to the traditions of human wisdom is leading more profoundly to a telling of and a listening to new stories that are both ancient and new, integrating the wisdom of ages with the tentative language and imagery of the yet to be born. A new ethic grounds the story/ies in the materiality of human and planetary existence while its enactment in ritual/s sustains the journey. Fidelity to the telling of and listening to the new story/ies in all their dimensions and processes will ensure the dawning of a new day that can only yet be glimpsed in the creative imagination.

Notes

1. Diarmuid O'Murchu, *Reclaiming Spirituality* (New York: Crossroad, 1977), 19–20.

2. It is this that an ancient psalmist of Israel envisioned:

> Steadfast love and faithfulness will meet;
> righteousness and peace will kiss each other.
> Faithfulness will spring up from the ground,
> and righteousness will look down from the sky.
> (Ps. 85:10–11)

3. Joan Chittister's *In Search of Belief* (Liguori, Mo.: Liguori/Triumph, 1999) is an example of one such new story. In it she engages the Nicene Creed in the context of the shifts in consciousness and religious/spiritual awareness to which this essay has made reference.

4. These latter perspectives are characteristic of the principles for the Earth Bible, a multivolume project edited by Norman Habel of Adelaide, Australia, whose first volume is to be published by Sheffield Academic Press in 2000, and which is exemplary of the telling of the new story within a renewed ecological consciousness.

5. From the address "Love and Social Justice" given by bell hooks to the American Academy of Religion meeting in Boston, November 1999. Joan Chittister in her book *The Fire in These Ashes: A Spirituality of Contemporary Religious Life* (Kansas City, Mo.: Sheed & Ward, 1995) places the "call to love" at the heart of the religious or spiritual quest and journey.

24

Globalization and the Perennial Question of Justice

Mary John Mananzan, OSB

Introduction

After reflecting on the question posed by the editor of this *Festschrift,* "What is the most important spiritual question of our time?" I have come to the conclusion that it still is the question of justice. I also find it fitting to write on this topic because this *Festschrift* is in honor of a woman passionately committed to justice. For a long time justice has been the preoccupation of the church and yet it is as urgent now as ever before. In our times this question of justice is, for me, tied up with a global phenomenon — globalization. In this essay I propose to clarify this elusive term, discuss its impact on the peoples of the third world, especially Asia, particularly the Philippines. I would then make some theological and ethical conclusions and see its impact on one's spirituality.

What Is Globalization?

It is very necessary to say exactly what we mean by the word "globalization," because so many things are meant by it. It can mean the worldwide development of technology that makes the world into the so-called global village. As such, we have nothing against this development. Some people will take it to mean the networking going on internationally in all fields, and if this is all that is meant, we also have nothing against it, because true international solidarity cannot but be positive. I would like to define it, however, in the context in which it arose — in its economic *Sitz im Leben.* In the 60s and 70s activists (including me) went into the streets to denounce "foreign control of the economy," "economic imperialism," and so on. Today, these words have become unpopular and yet the reality they describe is still very much with us but decked with the euphemistic word "globalization."

So generically, globalization means the integration of the economies of the world into the liberal market economy of the West controlled by the G8. Here are some of its main features:

1. *Borderless economy.* It advocates the elimination of protective tariffs and gives free play to the market.

2. *Import liberalization.* This is a corollary of the borderless economy. Goods from all other countries can enter our country. This may seduce us as consumers to think that it is good because then we have many choices and the competition can bring down the prices. But this will also kill local industries, and when they are killed we will be dependent for our basic needs on other countries and this certainly will not ensure, for example, food security. This is not sustainable consumption.

3. *Free play of the market.* This advocates less control from the state and making the market forces the main criteria of activities. This will make profit and market demand the supreme values. Everything else will be sacrificed to these — consumers, labor, and so on. This does away with social and ethical concerns.

4. *Privatization.* All productive enterprises will be put into private hands, and in our case, mostly foreign hands. This effectively entrenches the foreign control of our economy (Calabarzone controlled by Taiwanese, Lotto by Malaysians, textiles by Germans, and so on). This will also put basic services, such as energy, into private hands, whose motive is profit. Therefore, subsidies will have to be taken away and prices of basic services will soar.

5. *Financial capitalism.* Today, there is actually not much productivity going on in our country. What is going on is financial speculation. So even production is done not to serve needs but for speculation. The only two productions happening are textiles and electronics, but these depend upon imports for 80 percent of their components.

The result of this is an export-oriented, import-dependent, foreign-investment-controlled, and debt-ridden economy.

The Impact of Globalization on Peoples

Globalization is not a new phenomenon. As mentioned above, it is the euphemistic term for that we have fought against for many years:

the foreign control of our economy — in short, economic imperialism. But the new word is seductive because it promises so many things that would make a heaven on earth. And yet, when we look at the actual consequences of globalization, it is just the opposite.

Consider the crisis we are suffering in Asia. Barely five years ago Asian countries were supposed to be "tigers" and "cubs." Now, no Asian country, not even Japan, is spared a currency crisis, stock market crisis, food crisis, energy crisis, employment crisis, and so on.

Janet Bruin aptly observes,

> Instead of spreading wealth around, "globalization" and current macro-economic policies in both North and South are concentrating wealth in fewer hands. Unemployment and the number of people living in poverty are increasing in many countries. Workers are being forced into low paying jobs and women are being forced into unsafe workplaces, into the unprotected informal economy where social security and other benefits do not apply, or into prostitution. Children are forced to leave school for work in carpet factories, farms or in the streets to help support their families, and people are forced to leave their countries in search of paid labor elsewhere, provoking an international backlash against immigrants as economic and security threats. Both migration and anti-immigrant xenophobia are expected to intensify as population pressures, unemployment, and economic disparities between countries become ever more acute.[1]

This has lately been confirmed by the United Nations Development Program (UNDP), which has come up with a comprehensive report involving many countries of the third world, pointing to one uncontested fact: globalization has widened the gap between the rich and the poor.[2]

In the Philippines and in Asia conversion of fertile lands into golf courses and industrial complexes has reduced the land available for the cultivation of staple food. Some cultivated lands are reserved for cash crops like asparagus and cut flowers. This not only reduces lands available for cultivation of staple food for local consumption, but also causes adverse effects on soil fertility because of the massive use of fertilizers and pesticides. The Philippines now imports rice, whereas it provided that staple sufficiently for itself in the past. Lack of subsidy and technological help to farmers renders agriculture a nonsustainable activity and reduces farmers to amassing continuous debt. The proliferation of prawn farms and fishing pens for growing prawns and fish for export has allotted marine resources, which form part of the peoples' daily fare, to the export business.

Deregulation of the oil companies has caused them to raise the price of oil arbitrarily and, in a domino effect, that of all basic commodities. All this, plus the recent devaluation of the Philippine peso, has caused housewives to stretch their marketing money to the breaking point. Import liberalization tries to convince the consumer that this would mean more choices and cheaper prices in competition. But this eventually destroys local industries and local businesses, leading to the loss of food security because the consumers become dependent on foreign producers. The Chernobyl incident underlined the dependence of a lot of countries with regard to dairy products.

The Center for Women Resources study on the General Agreement of Tariffs and Trade (GATT) concludes,

> As our economy is oriented more and more towards producing "cash crops" and depending more and more on imports for basic staples such as rice and corn, sources of our daily food consumption become unstable, putting the very survival of the Filipinos at stake.[3]

So are we saying that no one is benefiting from globalization? Of course not! But the question is, Who benefits from it? The upper 2 percent who have capital. Maybe it trickles down to the 10 percent who are used in the management of the enterprises. And basic sectors are not only excluded from the gains of the economic activities going under globalization, but are also negatively affected by it. Homes of urban poor were violently demolished during the last Asia-Pacific Economic Cooperation (APEC) meeting hosted by the Philippines. Due to land conversions, thousands of Filipino farmers have been dispersed and have lost the lands they till. Indigenous people are suffering the loss of their ancestral lands due to mining. Further, the strip mining has polluted their rivers and seas, depriving them of still another source of living. Workers who are supposed to be the main beneficiaries of industrialization are now suffering the loss of job security because of contractual labor practices. And in all these sectors, women are the most adversely affected because of the feminization of poverty.

Globalization has no respect for the uniqueness of peoples' culture. It has successfully "macdonalized" or "cocalized" the world. Urban youth culture is a monoculture of discos, malls, and jeans. Indigenous culture is exploited and bastardized for tourists. So the effect of globalization is not only on our economic life but also on our culture. It also has political implications because the decision makers of international agencies like the IMF-WB, WTO, and GATT are not elected by people, yet their decisions adversely affect the lives of so many. Nicanor Perlas writes, "The posture of GATT is totalitarian and radically arrayed against any notion of sovereignty and self-determination."[4]

Theological and Ethical Reflections

When one looks at the effects of globalization on the majority of excluded peoples, one can conclude that it has unleashed forces of death. Pope John Paul II writes in *Solicitudo Rei Socialis,*

> In today's world, including the world of economics, the prevailing picture is one destined to lead us more quickly toward death rather than one of concern for true development which would lead all toward a "more human world" as envisaged by the encyclical *Populorum Progressio.*[5]

The Ecumenical Association of Third World Theologians (EATWOT) has drawn this same conclusion. Thus, it has made globalization its main concern in its last general assembly in December 1996 in Tagaytay, Philippines, with its theme "Search for a New Just World Order: Challenges to Theology." Moreover, it has adopted as its theological theme for the next five years, "Towards a Fullness of Life: Theology in the Context of Globalization."

In all the national, continental, and intercontinental meetings of EATWOT the members are urged to continue the theological reflection begun in the general assembly. In some theological reflections EATWOT members see globalization as a sort of "new religion." It has its God: profit and money. It has its high priests: GATT, WTO, IMF-WB. It has its doctrines and dogmas: import liberalization, deregulation, and so on. It has its temples: the super megamalls. It has its victims on the altar of sacrifice: the majority of the world — the excluded and marginalized poor.

In the face of globalization EATWOT sees the need for a prophetic theology

> that will critique prince and priest, market and mammon, multinationals and war merchants and all hegemony and all plunder of the poor. It will call into question the silence of religions and

churches as children die of hunger in Iraq, in Orissa, due to im-
perialist policies of superpowers or local magnates. It will call
into question the centuries old oppression of women at home
and in society. And it will seek to serve people's dreams and
struggles for a beautiful tomorrow.[6]

The values of globalization are also ethically questionable. Its fore-
most value of profit and market is definitely an example of "serving
mammon." It has commodified people, treating workers as merely
factors in production. This is shown by its policies of "flexibilization
of labor" and "labor-only contracting." Women and children are likewise commodities to be used in child labor or in sex trafficking. Its
practice of cutthroat competition, which even prevents governments
from protecting their fledgling industries, is an economic survival of
the fittest. This leads to the economic dictatorship of the rich and
powerful, who become even richer and more powerful. For globalization, people such as the urban poor, who do not have capital or
skills to be in the playing field, are totally expendable. Globalization
promotes consumerism by its aggressive advertising techniques and
by luring consumers with megamalls and supermarkets. It convinces
people that their wants are needs and that they have the right to buy
anything as long as they can afford it. This leads to surplus production, which has not only depleted our irreplaceable natural resources,
but also has caused ecological disasters such as deforestation, pollution, thinning of the ozone layer, global warming, and, with these,
the consequent "natural" calamities.

One ethically questionable issue that is connected with globalization is biotechnology or genetic engineering. Nicanor Perlas describes
it this way:

> This science and technology package is based on the belief that
> there is nothing sacred in life, that life is simply a bunch of
> chemicals (DNA and related compounds) and their interactions
> and that all traits — from chemical properties, outer appearance,
> and behaviour — can be understood and reconstructed on the
> basis of studies of the DNA and its manipulation. Human beings
> could now play God, disassembling, decoding, recombining all
> life forms on the planet.[7]

At present, tens of thousands of genetic experimentations are going on. Life forms have been patented, animals have been cloned, and
both open the ominous possibility of cloning human beings. With

GATT, activities of biopirates have been legitimized. Multinational companies go all over the world collecting precious plants and animal species, interfere with their genetic makeup, and patent them to the detriment of the peoples who had been using these for centuries for their livelihood. For the sake of profit, seeds are tampered with so that they cannot reproduce, forcing farmers to buy more seeds. Furthermore, science and technology are producing food products that are harmful, such as irradiated food, pesticide-laden products, and biotech food. Indeed, never before has the assault to life been as massive as in our times. Economics cannot continue to be immune from moral and ethical scrutiny. The tremendous injustice, exclusion of peoples, and assault to life resulting from globalization must be morally judged and condemned. The opposite values of sharing, service, compassion, equity, interdependence, and solidarity must be reemphasized.

Spirituality for Our Times

In order to face the challenges of today, we need to develop a spirituality attuned to our times. There are several characteristics of this spirituality.

1. It is a *prophetic spirituality*. It is a spirituality that is convinced of the good news it has to announce and has the courage to denounce what it considers as the bad news. There are many people who are more convinced that God wants us to suffer than that God wants us to be happy. We somehow have to convey to people that God wants them to be truly happy in an integral way, meaning body and soul. When we see obstacles to this integral salvation of peoples, we must not hesitate to take a stand, even if this would mean risks or inconveniences for us. In other words, it is a committed spirituality. In our times it is a commitment to economic justice, gender and racial equality, and ecological activism.

2. It is an *integral spirituality*. Just as we proclaim an integral salvation, we also have to develop an integral spirituality that transcends dichotomies such as body-soul, sacred-profane, contemplation-action, heaven-earth, and so on. We need to integrate our relationships with God, with ourselves, with others, and with the planet. It is inclusive and resists exclusion of peoples for any reason, be it class, race, gender, or any other.

3. It is a spirituality that is characterized by *simplicity of lifestyle.* In contrast to consumerism, it strives to do without superfluities, mindful that the earth's resources are limited and that these have to be shared by all.

4. It is an *empowering spirituality.* It is self-affirming, aware, and grateful for God's gifts to us giving us a healthy self-esteem. It is also mutually empowering, affirming other people and facilitating their blossoming.

5. It is a *healing spirituality.* It is a process of healing one's own wounds and using one's own experiences to heal others.

6. It is a *contemplative spirituality.* It emphasizes moments of reflection, meditation, and contemplation — being present to the Presence, a constant awareness of the absolute within us, who is the inexhaustible source of joy, love, and energy and makes us committed but carefree.

7. It is an *Easter spirituality.* It is a spirituality that transcends Good Friday, that is infected with the fearless joy of Easter. It resists the forces of death and promotes the enhancement of life. It feasts more than it fasts. It is not so much control as surrender. It is not cold asceticism but a celebration of life.

Conclusion

The need is urgent to restore justice and harmony in human relationships at all levels and the relationship of human beings to the whole of creation. The continuing resistance of peoples' organizations against the forces of death in our society is a sign of hope. Christians have options. They can be obstacles to these efforts, bystanders, and let history move without them. Or, they can accompany the struggling peoples on their journey to the new Jerusalem, and together with them build a new heaven and a new earth.

Notes

1. Janet Bruin, *Root Causes of the Global Crisis* (Manila: Institute of Political Economy, 1996), 11.

2. *Human Development Report* (New York and Oxford: Oxford University Press, 1995).

thinking." I felt that it was very important to be at the Nevada test site at the beginning of the new millennium to denounce the way of thinking that justified the development and the use of these weapons of mass destruction during the past century and to proclaim a commitment to enter the new century with the strongest possible determination to change our way of thinking, leading to the total abolition of these weapons.

This is a matter of the greatest urgency. By threatening the total destruction of the world and all its people we are, in fact, destroying ourselves spiritually. In *The Challenge of Peace,* the pastoral letter of the U.S. Catholic bishops written in 1983, we stated, "The nuclear age is an era of moral as well as physical danger. We are the first generation since Genesis with the power to threaten the created order." It is almost impossible to grasp the full dimension of the evil that is contained in the intent to use nuclear weapons. Such an act is the most complete repudiation of God that we as human creatures could ever do. God is love, St. John says so plainly, and Jesus revealed so clearly when he "pitched his tent among us." God's love is manifest to us through God's creative power. All of the universe, our world, and each human person is loved into existence by God.

But nuclear weapons are a direct challenge to God's creative love. An Indian writer, Arundahti Roy, put it this way: "The nuclear bomb is the most antidemocratic, antinational, antihuman, outright evil thing that man has ever made. If you are religious, then remember that this bomb is man's challenge to God. It's worded quite simply. We have the power to destroy everything that You have created."[1] And to emphasize the physical danger hanging over us, she goes on to say, "If you're not [religious], then look at it this way. This world of ours is four thousand six hundred million years old. It could end in an afternoon."[2]

If you feel that the nuclear threat is over because the Cold War is over, you should know that such an afternoon was within ten minutes of happening on January 25, 1995. Russian military radar detected the launch of a U.S. scientific rocket from a base in Norway, and mistakenly concluded that it might be the beginning of a surprise attack. President Yeltsin was notified and given less than ten minutes to choose from a range of responses that included launching four thousand nuclear warheads against the U.S. What happened in Moscow that morning is not exactly clear, but fortunately the Russians did not launch a nuclear attack. The next time we may not be so lucky.[3]

With thirty-five thousand nuclear warheads in the world, and more than five thousand of these warheads in the U.S. and Russian arsenals on hair-trigger alert, there will be a next time. At some point these weapons will be launched on purpose or accidentally. The world will be over.

As terrifying as this inevitability is, I am even more concerned about our spiritual well-being. We are living in sin, the very sin described above: the direct repudiation of God's creative love. There can be no more total turning against God.

Am I exaggerating? I am convinced that I am not. Between 1981 and 1983 I served on the bishops' committee that developed the pastoral letter *The Challenge of Peace*. I remember so clearly the words of Gerard Smith, then the director of the Arms Control Agency: "There is no such thing as a strategy of deterrence without the clear intent to use the weapons." As a nation we are committed to this strategy. We sin when we form the clear intention to do evil. The subsequent action adds to the gravity of the sin and brings other consequences. But the sin is already there once we have determined to do it. And the clear intent to do it was confirmed in a conversation with Casper Weinberger, then our secretary of defense. In response to a question about the intent of our nation's policy he told us, "Of course, we don't want to do it. But when we have to, we will."

Do you wonder why there is so much violence in the United States? Why there are so many abortions? Why so many executions? So many people incarcerated in a brutal prison system? Why grade school and high school youngsters plot to kill and actually do kill their classmates? Why we have such a negligence toward the poor, the mentally ill, the homeless? Why we can heartlessly bring about the killing of thousands of poor people in an attack against Panama, ironically named Operation Just Cause? Why we could wage "low-intensity warfare" in Nicaragua, Guatemala, El Salvador, Haiti, and other places, bringing about the disappearance, the torture, and the killing of hundreds of thousands of innocent people? Why we have a policy resulting in the killing of one-half to three-quarters of a million children in Iraq through weapons of mass destruction and have our secretary of state declare, "It is worth it"? Richard McSorley, SJ, gave the answer many years ago. He declared that our intent to use nuclear weapons is the root cause of the violence in our society.

My judgment is that we are in danger of losing our souls. While we have become a "superpower" and are clearly the richest nation in all of history, we must ask ourselves at what price we have achieved this. It is past time for us to face the question Jesus posed: What does it profit anyone if you gain the whole world but suffer the loss of your soul?

We are at this point. The most important spiritual challenge we face is to begin a profound conversion. We must repent of our past sins, especially the sin of the original use of nuclear weapons. We must denounce and reject the continued intent to use such weapons. And we must energetically work for the total abolition of such weapons from the face of the earth.

Henri Nouwen began his book *The Living Reminder* with a story about Elie Wiesel.

> In 1944, all the Jews of the Hungarian town of Sighet were rounded up and deported to concentration camps. Elie Wiesel, the now famous novelist, was one of them. He survived the holocaust and twenty years later returned to see his hometown again. What pained him most was that the people of Sighet had erased the Jews from their memory. He writes: "I was not angry with the people of Sighet...for having driven out their neighbors of yesterday, nor for having denied them. If I was angry at all it was for having forgotten them. So quickly, so completely...Jews have been driven not only out of town but out of time as well."[4]

Then he goes on to make a very important application of the event to our current situation.

> This story suggests that to forget our sins may be an even greater sin than to commit them. Why? Because what is forgotten cannot be healed and that which cannot be healed easily becomes the cause of greater evil. In his many books about the holocaust, Elie Wiesel does not remind us of Auschwitz, Buchenwald, and Treblinka to torture our consciences with heightened guilt feelings, but to allow our memories to be healed and so to prevent an even worse disaster. An Auschwitz that is forgotten causes a Hiroshima, and a forgotten Hiroshima can cause the destruction of our world. By cutting off our past we paralyze our future: forgetting the evil behind us we evoke the evil in front of us. As George Santayanna has said: "He who forgets the past is doomed to repeat it."[5]

The evil we are evoking is the end of the world and the loss of our souls. Confronting this is the greatest spiritual question of our time.

Notes

1. Arundahti Roy, "The End of Imagination," *The Nation* (September 28, 1998): 19.

2. Ibid.

3. Physicians for Social Responsibility, "The Bomb — It Hasn't Gone Away," *Daily Hampshire Gazette* (December 1998): 5.

4. Henri J. M. Nouwen, *The Living Reminder* (San Francisco: HarperSan-Francisco, 1984), 17.

5. Ibid.

Afterword

The Power of Questions to Propel

A Retrospective

Joan Daugherty Chittister, OSB

Almost twenty-five hundred years ago the philosopher Plato wrote one of the most commonly cited dictums in the English language. "The unexamined life," he said, "is not worth living." The statement has been repeated almost to the point of oblivion. It recurs and recurs and recurs. It is, it seems, always there on the edge of the mind, taunting us to ask the questions that will explain us to ourselves, tempting us to dare the answers. Here, clearly, is an insight that the world knows to be important. It carries a truth — a challenge — that clings like a tick to the human soul. And yet, it takes years to understand it completely, perhaps. The longer I live, the more convinced I become of the fundamental truth of it, the more I wonder at the same time how many people really — consciously — rummage the ground, search out the underpinnings of the lives they lead. After all, it's a dangerous process.

There is something quite frightening about looking at the truisms of our lives and wondering how true they really are. To examine what is and find it wanting could threaten the boggy shoals on which we stand. The tidal wave called Truth could sweep in, then, and wash it all away. What if I look and find that there are tiny little fissures, obscure little lacunae in the systems on which I have staked my life? What if my country is not what I was told it was? What if my church itself is not free of sin? What if the laws are immoral? What if my truths are not true? — there is no Santa Claus; we are not the center of the universe; people do not go to hell because they ate meat on Friday; racial differences are not determinative; sexuality and gender neither enhance nor diminish a person. Then what do I do to go on walking the ruts of my road; what do I follow blindly to cure my own blindness; what do I do to grapple my soul to the ground of my growing? Then what shall I believe in when only belief can save me? I heard of a woman who, finding herself drifting toward the middle of a dangerously feminist conversation, stopped the group in the midst of the process. "I don't want to hear any more about any of this," she said, "because if I did, I would have to change my life." A wise woman. It is always so much easier to assuage pain than to cure it, so much easier to accept a thing than to question it.

This book is dedicated to the questions of the age to come, but this reflection is dedicated to the questions that brought me to this one. It is an exercise in the power of questions. It recognizes the necessity of questions to test the truth of our own lives. Without experience in a culture of questions we become the pawns of every period, however noble, however muffling of the human spirit it may be. Just because a thing does not seem to need to be questioned does not make the question ignoble. To be blind in darkness is every bit as bad as to be blind in the light. To be blind when everyone else is unseeing is every bit as bad as to be blind when everyone else is sighted.

The ability — the commitment — to question, to examine every aspect of the human journey is the only form of fidelity worth the price of admission to this sojourn called life. Otherwise, no sector of the social anatomy to which we swear emotional allegiance can trust us to serve it well. It is the questions we ask that moves us from stage to stage of our growing, that takes us from level to level of our thoughts, however simple the questions may seem. I have just realized, in fact, how boring my own questions have been over the years: Do non-Catholics go to heaven? Is sin the center of life? Or to put it another way, What is a "good" life? Does what we give up in life make for more holiness than what we do? Is religious life incarnational or transcendent? Don't we really need to be violent sometimes? What is a woman? Can a woman be Catholic? (No mention, you notice, of birth control, which also had a lot to do with radicalizing me, or divorce, which I have always believed in, even when it was a sin, or "the role of women in the home" which I knew was wrong by the time I was five.) And yet, without those questions there was no coming beyond the naïve simplicity of all the early answers to them: Only Catholics go to heaven. Sins are the things against the law, and the purpose of life is to avoid them. Good things are bad for you. Or — the second version — really good people give up good things. Religious life requires separation from "the world." The Crusades and Vietnam were noble ventures fought to make the world safe for Christianity. Woman is man's helpmate. The reason women can't minister to the people of God sacramentally is because God wants it that way.

It was an age of absolute certainty in the face of growing complexities. It was an age that absolutely dismissed questions. It was an age that needed questions badly but had been forbidden to ask them.

We each have our own personal set of questions. For those of us who lived the greater part of the twentieth century — during the wars, before and after Vatican II, in the midst of the second wave of the woman's movement — maybe the questions I find so mundane today were common ones. Maybe they were quite different from the ones asked by the people around me. But whatever the ilk of them, the process of writing them out — like this — is a humbling experience. It exposes the level of inquiry with which a life has been consumed. It also unmasks the questions behind the questions that agitate the very pilings of the world around me.

At the same time, it is a worthwhile excursion into the soul to look at the questions that have shaped our lives and ask what it was about them that intrigued us in the first place, that changed us as we dealt with them, that brought me, as a result of them, to be the person that I am today. After all, it is only in the light of our past that we understand the present with which we grapple as well the future toward which we strive.

But questions never exist in a vacuum. Or at least they never get answered in one. They happen when Galileo finds himself fascinated by these particular swinging lampstands in this particular church and then begins to time them by his own pulse rate. They happen when Columbus comes ashore on the wrong island in the wrong sea. They happen when something vital founders in our own lives. My own questions of the last half of the twentieth century did not come out of textbooks. They came out of the protean pieces of what was otherwise a quite ordinary paradigm: I was Irish Roman Catholic, woman, religious. Those were the filters through which I saw my world. The questions that emerged out of each of them were, by any means of measure, few. But they changed me completely.

What Kind of God Is This?

My Irish Catholic mother was a very young widow when she remarried. I was five years old. Dutch Chittister, my new father, had been raised Presbyterian, but churchgoing had had little meaning to him. He liked to show me the small Bible he'd been awarded for perfect Sunday school attendance, of course, but I never saw him read it and I never, ever, heard him talk about anything in it. He went to the local parish priest for marriage preparation discussions as a concession to my mother, but the thought of his continuing with instructions in the

faith was not out of the question. He was, after all, not intensely committed to any tradition, and "mixed" marriages were not anyone's
definition of the ideal relationship.

Fr. O'Connell, the parish priest, was the stern, dogmatic type. No
foolishness allowed. Instructions were basic and direct. You either
believed or you didn't. "To be saved," he taught, "it is necessary to be
Catholic." My new father seemed suddenly alert. "Wait a minute,"
he paused the process. "Are you saying that my mother didn't go
to heaven when she died?" O'Connell pushed the pamphlet across
the table. "You can read," he said. "Read it yourself." My mother,
years later, was still saying that it might not have been nearly so bad
if the priest had just not shoved the pamphlet so hard. Dutch got
up out of his chair, suddenly, harshly. His face burned red. "You're
completely mad," he said tautly. "I'm leaving this place." Then he
looked at my mother. "Make up your mind. Are you leaving with me
or staying with him?" She reached out and picked up her coat. They
never talked about his taking instructions again and our family life
changed drastically from what it might have been.

Somehow or other, the two of them figured out how to negotiate
the problem, but the question stayed with me forever. What was at
stake here? His salvation? My grandmother's salvation? Yes, but far
more than that. What was really at stake was the kind of God who
would create a world full of people who had come thousands of years
before Christ and thousands of years after Christ and decree that
belief in Christ was essential to their souls. What was at stake was
the fact that these people, too, were religious, were good, were holy.
What was at stake was faith in a God who would create a world in
order to damn the greater part of its inhabitants through no fault of
their own.

I had two problems. The first was that I simply could not believe in
a sadistic God. The second was that so much evil had been done in the
name of conversion to the true faith — starting in the great religious
conversion campaigns and ending, for me as a small child, in that
rectory. In the final analysis I found it harder to believe in a hierarchical heaven where some people are "higher" than other people than I
did to believe that everyone is meant to enjoy whatever heaven itself
might be. But how is it possible to deal with such problems when the
law of your life says otherwise? It took a while.

I spent years awash in values that made the parochial the ultimate.
But after years of *lectio,* years of immersion in Scripture, years of
a monasticism that predated the divisions in the church and so was
naturally ecumenical, what finally saved me from a faith too small

was the memory of the Jesus who talked to Caananite women and who sent Samaritans to speak his name to a different people in a different way. There was, I came to see, no mention in Scripture that the Samaritans who came to believe in him became Jews. Like my father, they stayed Samaritan, it seemed.

The question of heaven, of God, of truth led me to realize that if God is truly a creating God, a loving God, we all have a special role in God's design. I began to seek out what there was to learn, to appreciate of God, in each religion around me and, eventually, in every religion everywhere. Vatican II, with its insight that we were to respect "all that was good and true" in non-Christian religions, brought me beyond Fr. O'Connell to the center of my own soul, where the God of creation waited to give me into the embrace of the entire world, to teach me a more total truth. I came to realize that the more I learned about differences in all things, the more I would understand myself in all my weaknesses, all my strengths. As the years went by and I began to work with Buddhists and meet Bahai and talk with Muslims, I also began to recognize that coming from a "mixed" marriage — a marriage where truth came in different designs — was one of the graces of my life.

Is Sin the Center of Life?

I was a young nun. Everyone in the novitiate was near the same age, most of us just out of high school, some of us not yet graduated. The early days in the convent were a panoply of interesting things: veils to adjust and office books to mark, stiff ways to walk and new ways to eat, silence to keep and books to read. There was only one major problem: when the confessor came every Wednesday, no one in the novitiate wanted to go. I remember slipping from the head of the line to the back of it over and over again. When the rest of the line had been exhausted and I couldn't avoid the situation anymore, I simply remember saying to the priest, "Bless me, Father, for I have sinned — but to tell you the truth I haven't been here long enough to do anything." I heard him shift in the box. I shifted too. Someplace inside of me, I knew that something was seriously wrong, all right, but it was not the things they'd told me.

The whole context of sin had changed for me. Was it really "sin" to break silence, or eat between meals, or speak to people on the street, or keep a gift box of candy rather than hand it in to the novice mistress? Each week we "spoke fault" for being human: spilling things, walking heavily, eating between meals. I admit that I never really repented any of them, but I became more and more aware of the weakness of the self and less and less aware of its glory. Life was one long slippery slope away from God.

Sin had become the center of a life that the presence of God was supposed to occupy. What we did — the silly, schoolgirl peccadilloes — rather than what we failed to do — became the focus of the spiritual life. I once heard Fulton Sheen say, "My fear for the religious of the church is that they will be fit only for the sandboxes of heaven." It was a chilling thought. It was also a very real one.

The Korean War, McCarthyism, and trade union problems came and went, but we knew very little about them because reading newspapers was forbidden. Someone was making sure that "worldliness" would not creep into us. As a result, nothing crept in that was touching the lives of the world around us — not the deep political tensions, not the great atomic questions, not the first soundings of the racial divide, not the tentacles of militarism that were strengthening their chokehold on U.S. society. We were oblivious to it all. We said not a word as a community about any of it.

All the time we worried about sin we had lost a sense of what it really was. We had managed to confuse the moral, the immoral, and the amoral. We were learning, literally, to be good for nothing. Religious life, however well intentioned, had become little more than a relic of the proclamations of Palestine, the memory of martyrdoms no longer tolerated, a mental construct of great gospel valor without a skeleton to hang it on.

When Pope John XXIII talked about "the signs of the times" — poverty, nuclearism, sexism — I began to read these signs with a new conscience and with a new sense of religious life in mind. Most of all, I began to read the Scriptures through another lens. Who was this Jesus who "consorted with sinners" and cured on the Sabbath? Most of all, who was I who purported to be following him while police dogs snarled at black children and I made sure not to be late for prayer or leave my monastery after dark? What was the "prophetic dimension" of the church supposed to be about if not the concerns of the prophets? — the widows, the orphans, the foreigners, and the broken, vulnerable of every society.

We prayed the psalms five times a day for years, but I had failed to hear them. What I heard in those early years of religious life was the need to pray. I forgot to hear what I was praying. Then, one day I realized just how secular the psalmist was in comparison to the religious standards in which I had been raised: "You, O God, do see trouble and grief.... You are the helper of the weak," the psalmist argues. No talk of warm, fuzzy religion here. This was life raw and hard. This was what God called to account (Ps. 10:14). This was sin.

When the Latin American bishops talked about a "fundamental option for the poor," I began to see the poor in our inner-city neighborhood for the first time. When Rosa Parks and Martin Luther King Jr. finally stood up in Birmingham, Alabama, I stood up too. I was ready now. Like the blind man of Mark's Gospel, I could finally see. The old question had been answered. The sin to be repented, amended, and eradicated was the great systemic sin against God's little ones. For that kind of sin, in my silence, I had become deeply guilty.

I had new questions then but they were far more energizing than the ones before them. I began to look more closely at what "living a good life" could possibly mean in a world that was so full of suffering, so full of greed.

I began to realize that a "good life" had something do with making life good for other people. Slowly, slowly, I began to arrive at the oldest Catholic truth of them all: all of life is good and sanctity does not consist in denying that. Sanctity consists in making life good for everyone whose life we touch. I began to understand the most ancient parts of the monastic tradition. In the "Apothegmata: The Sayings of the Desert Monastics" we hear of a monk whom the people criticized for breaking his fast to eat and drink with visitors. They wanted him condemned. Instead, the holy ones of the area commended him in public for breaking the laws of the monastic life in order to keep the law of God to love the other. I began to see newly, to see differently, to see with an open heart. Giving things up was one thing; getting them for other people was something else. To be a religious in this world I would need to treat the world religiously — with reverence, with love, with joy. To "be in it but not of it" as Jesus was, I could see now, was a far greater mandate than "thou shalt not." No more "symbolic" gestures in the name of commitment, no more praying with outstretched arms to assure myself that I, too, was living a crucified life, no more playacting religion would do. Now it was time to ask some real-life questions and to say my own answers to them aloud so that others could find the arena in which they might add their own.

The question "What is sin?" had changed my life completely. I had discovered the ones I should have been confessing when I was a novice. I came to understand that selfishness, self-centeredness, and the kind of self-indulgence that is bought at the expense of the other was the real essence of sin. The private little wrestling matches, the pitfalls that come and go with the process of personal development, were all part of our secret struggles to resist the predisposition to sin that is part of being human. Those were all part of the growing up process, yes, but it was not of the real essence of either sin or sanctity. Sanctity had far more to do with building up the reign of God here and now for everyone. All the saints were "sinners" in the narcissistic sense of the word. But all the saints were also those who overturned tables in every temple of every system in which exploiting the little ones of the world was one of the givens of the social game. Since God lives in all of us, the destruction of the other has to be a sin against God.

I had discovered that life was for the living and that to live a good life meant that we had to live it in such a way that we made it even better for everyone else.

What Is Holy Violence?

I was a graduate student at Penn State when the word came. A young cousin, Norman Chittister, had been killed in Vietnam just before his twenty-first birthday and two weeks away from being discharged. He would have been best man at his best friend's marriage one week later. Instead, he would be buried in the family plot at the end of the week. He was an only child. I was on my way to the funeral.

The Vietnam War was raging all around me on the campus at the time. Young men who were in class one week had left the country for Canada by the next in order to escape the draft. I never took part in any demonstrations but I watched mystified as the silent candlelight parades passed nightly down College Avenue under my dormitory window. Students disrupted classes, streaked naked across lecture halls carrying antiwar slogans, smoked marijuana and dyed their long hair green, as if all the moral standards they'd been given had simply come to boil, gone to pus, and erupted all over the generation before them that had concentrated on private piety but failed to recognize public sin. What was happening to patriotism? To obedience? To the defense of democracy? I passed through the main gates of the university every day — on my way to class, of course — as they read the names of the war dead in one unending monotone day and night, day and night, day and night for weeks. I was getting my doctorate. I had no time for the political rebellion of naturally rebellious youth.

I was also a child of World War II, the "good war," the war between the forces of freedom and a ruthless, genocidal dictator. We had won a "holy war." We were the Messianic People, the City on the Hill, the New Jerusalem. We had saved the world for democracy and were now girding to repel atheistic communism, as well, something every Catholic child dreaded far more than we did Hitler. Hitler would make us Germans, yes, but communism would make us godless.

In the end, we failed in Korea and we failed in Vietnam, but both failure and success in war looked the same on American soil. We had done it all totally untouched, completely unscathed, without a scar — or so we wanted to believe. War was something that most Americans saw in Saturday matinees and on Gold Stars in old ladies' windows. Americans won wars without blood, without gore. And we did it with honor, we were taught. But then began the dismantling of the myths, the beginning of the questions.

I remember where I was standing when Dwight D. Eisenhower, past war hero, then president of the United States, admitted on television that he had lied to the American people when he denied that Gary Powers and his U-2 airplane were flying spy missions over the Soviet Union. What seems almost laughable now, paltry, innocent, was almost unthinkable then. We did not spy. Presidents did not lie to the people. We would not invade the airspace of another sovereign nation with intent to intrude. But we had.

I remember discovering that Japan had tried to surrender at the end of World War II and that we had ignored their diplomatic advances in order to "experiment" with not one, but two, nuclear weapons, now euphemistically called "nuclear devices."

I remember learning that Lyndon B. Johnson had made up a story of hostile and continuing action in the Bay of Tonkin in order to justify an all-out attack on Vietnam, with the loss of American lives as well as Vietnamese. I remember, most of all, the release of the Pentagon Papers and the trail of deception they told of U.S. secret involvement in Southeast Asia.

I remember realizing with horror that we were not at war against soldiers anywhere anymore. We were at war with the entire civilian populations of those places, old men and babies, deaf grandmothers and pregnant women.

At the funeral parlor with the family, I searched for words of comfort for a grieving aunt and uncle whose only child was being used to bolster a political system that was being untrue to its own ideals. But before I could say a word, my uncle said strongly, "Well, at least we're the lucky ones. Our son was a hero, not one of those traitors on a college campus." I stood at the coffin and gave myself all the old answers, but none of them worked.

Soon after Norman's funeral, elsewhere in the United States, soldiers shot into a crowd of American students on an American campus while babies ran through the streets of Vietnam aflame in napalm. At the same time, one of my best friends, a young nun, was arrested for being part of a sit-in at one of the companies that supplied the chemicals. The questions stirred in my heart and no amount of patriotism, of "obedience," could quiet them. The questions grated against a part of the human soul that I had never before realized I had.

We had become what we hated. And we were prepared to do it again. "Mutually assured destruction," the commitment to a nuclear first strike if we ourselves feared being struck — to destroy first what might destroy us — was the order of the day. It was called a "deterrent" but it had already started to kill people everywhere, even here, by virtue of the funds it took away from education and medicine and housing and food.

I questioned the value of the war; I questioned the effectiveness of violence; I questioned the integrity of the country; I questioned the theology of the church. Most of all, I remembered the Jesus who told Peter to put away his sword and went to his death killing no one on the way.

Life became a nightmare of contradictions. Prayer became a searing truth. How was it possible to "love your enemies" and then set out consciously, designedly, to annihilate them? "We had to destroy this village in order to save it," the papers quoted a commander as saying by way of explanation for the rout of civilian rice growers in the Asian farmland. I struggled between the church of the martyrs and the church of the crusaders. Violence was clearly not the road to love. Violence was clearly not the way of Jesus. Where were we as a church in the middle of this? How could we teach one thing and say not a public word about the other on the pretext of the separation of church and state? Is that what silenced us during the Holocaust, too? How could any of this be "holy"?

Exhausted by the spiritual wrenching that came with having lived through a "good war" and now watching as we ourselves conducted an evil one, I became part of a Christian peace movement that challenged the continuing viability of any theory of a just war in a world where disproportionality was now official government policy and discrimination in targeting a theological joke. The questions simply would not, could not, quit in me. The personal effects of the spiritual scuffle were cataclysmic for me.

Once a standard-brand U.S. Roman Catholic, I now found myself inside some new circles and outside some old ones. I was suddenly considered "radical" to most, "communist" to some, at best "misguided" to many, including priests who previously had called me "a good sister." But there was no turning back. The gentle Jesus of my daily prayer was far too clear to be ignored at a time of social convenience. I found myself certain that though conflict resolution might not be able to guarantee peace, violence certainly could not. After Selma and South Africa, Kosovo and Bosnia, I knew that my questions had brought me to a whole new place in both church and state. Violence launched for the sake of political ends was a sin. It lurked under false pretenses of honor and righteousness but it was evil. And the seed of it lived in my own soul or no government would ever be able to tap it there so easily for the sake of its crusades and inquisitions and carpet bombings and ethnic cleansings and genocides.

Systemic violence was not holy, and I could not support any country that was doing it, not even my own; and further, Scripture showed me quite clearly, never, ever, could I give such support in the name of Jesus.

What Is a Woman?

I grew up on stories. Every night my mother and father took turns telling me a bedtime story. I was in fourth grade before the process finally tapered off to a halt and I began reading my own. But over the years I had developed a list of favorites out of the repertoire, which I requested over and over again. In one of them my mother told the story of the only black family in the small, all-white Pennsylvania hill town in which she grew up. My entire family, including my grandfather, was quarantined because one of the many children had some kind of childhood disease. No one could go out and no one could come in. It was a desperate time. With no money to count on and grandfather's job in jeopardy if he didn't return to it quickly, grandma was scrimping on everything. His was the only income, the only support.

Then one day, Mamie Galloway, the black woman from the other side of the dam and the mother of a large family herself, who seldom, if ever, ventured into town, showed up on Donegal Hill in front of our house. She was carrying a basket. "Come out, madam," she shouted to my grandmother, who was watching from the front window. "I'll roll these eggs down the porch one at a time. You catch them carefully." Mamie Galloway kept a garden and raised chickens. "Where did she get those chickens?" I asked myself again and again as I listened to the story. The white man's business and labor problems meant nothing to her. Mamie Galloway supported herself.

Every day for the duration of the quarantine Mamie Galloway
came with a dozen eggs and rolled them down the porch to grandma
and never charged a penny. An independent black woman. A black, a
woman, who was independent. And she rolled them, free, to us. "And
that, Joan," my mother always said at the end of the story, "means
that prejudice is wrong. Everyone is good and everyone is capable.
You must always accept everyone. And you must always do your best
whether people accept you or not." It was a story about prejudice,
true. But only on one level. How to account for Mamie Galloway
herself was my problem.

I learned early on that some people, whatever their talents,
whatever their goodness, ranked lower than other people in life. I
discovered that "Irish need not apply," that there were "black water
fountains" and "white lunch counters." And, I learned, it was wrong.
But it took me awhile to realize that I was one of them.

Women, someone somewhere had decided, were simply not as intelligent, not as strong, not as emotionally stable as men. Who could
possibly say that my grandmother, who bore thirteen children and
ran a house on nothing and lived to be eighty-three, was not strong?
And who could say that my mother, who was a self-made doctor and
smarter than any man I ever knew, who buried two husbands and
went on alone despite it, was not strong, not stable, not intelligent?
But they had to struggle, I knew, for the right to cast a vote, to go
to school, to support themselves when the husbands on whom they
were required to depend for their survival were no longer with them.
What about a woman's abilities, I wondered? Why didn't they count
in the great national reservoir of talent?

My mother, undereducated and dependent all her life, trained me
fiercely for independence. What she could not have, she wanted for
me. I got no speeches about "woman's role" and "women's place"
from her. Instead, I got a vision and a direction. I was to study hard
so that I could "take care of myself." I was to realize that I could do
"anything I set my mind to." I was to understand that I was a person
first, and possibly, but not necessarily, a mother as well.

But it was a schizophrenic situation. At home I was geared for
equality. I went fishing with my father, laid a roof or two, helped
plan the family budget, and, in the idiom of the time, studied hard to
"get ahead." But in the world around me, I was only a girl. And girls
did not get ahead; my mother was my own best proof of that. Boys
led the band. Boys played sports. Boys became doctors. Boys made
the money. Boys traveled. Boys became politicians. Boys had clubs
and businesses and fishing trips and adventures. Boys did it all. And

whatever the talents of a girl, eventually she put them all down to be "a woman."

Suppressing part of the human community for the sake of its other parts was not a new trick. But everywhere men controlled the system and everywhere men taught other men that such was the way it should be. When other races, peoples, and nations were freed, women were never completely freed. What they got to do in society, if they got to do much at all, they did by virtue of concession or necessity, not by reason of human right. Women were allowed to get jobs because there weren't enough men there to take them. Women were allowed to go to school because men needed educated women to support their industries. Women, for the most part, were relegated to the home because raising children "was the most important thing a person could do in life." But if it was really so important, why weren't men doing their share of it?

The question I grew up with in the center of my soul was, Why all this? Why this diminishment of women? Unfortunately, the question has not really changed. Today, women are still being beaten, enslaved, raped, murdered, and married into intolerable degradation simply because they are women. Around the world girl babies are routinely aborted or abandoned. In Bombay, at the dawn of the twenty-first century, technology makes it easier to select the sex of a child. Over 250 amniocentesis/abortion centers advertise in their windows how to avoid the burdens of paying the dowry that comes with bearing the unwanted female child: "Spend 700 rupees now and save the 700,000 rupees later," the signs say. The woman who does not deal with the woman's question, if not for herself, for women everywhere, has yet, I came to understand, to really become a woman. But she does not know it.

The question that grew to burn in me was, To whose advantage, for what purpose, on what authority are women defined as the domestics of society? The Mamie Galloways of the world had discovered how to live outside the system, yes, had proved they were worth their salt, had shown their strength. And that was not enough. That was only a symbol, a sign, of what could be, should be, must be if humanity is ever to be wholly human.

These questions were my questions. Either I had to deal with them or know that my life had failed — not only my own life, my mother's, and my grandmother's, but all the daughters of all our days. It was my life or theirs, and since the questions were mine, the answer was obvious. I simply did not believe anymore in the natural inferiority of women, whatever the male theology of depreciation taught me to revere about men and reject about me. What we had was the social diminishment of one half the human race for the sake of the other, and yet, ironically, to the peril of them both. The God who would create half of humanity to be half as good as the other half, half as whole as the other half, is a teasing, taunting bully. Not my God. Not the God who created all humanity as "bone of my bone, flesh of my flesh, somebody just like me." Not the God who looked at humanity and said, "That's good." Not "some" are good. Or some are "half good." I must believe, then, that women are really fully human, human beings. And, to be true to the theology of creation, I must contest any system that teaches otherwise.

Can a Woman Be Catholic?

We were at a meeting in Rome. "We" were a mixed group of men and women religious. The 250 men were in the midst of their regular international congress, the sessions at which the standards of the order for both women and men were defined and its theology developed. The twelve women were the first women observers ever admitted to the meeting. Tours were planned to acquaint the abbots with various monasteries in the area, all more or less associated with the history of the group. Lunch was planned at the major site of the trip. When the bell rang, the group proceeded toward the refectory. But when the women reached the door, the porter closed it in their faces. The men, he explained, went into the main community dining room; a lunch had been prepared for the women elsewhere, but no one was quite sure where. The problem, he explained to us, was "cloister." But if the privacy of the community was the issue, I asked, why were the men allowed to break it but not the women? And why, in the women's monastery we had visited before this one, were men allowed to be present there if we were not allowed to be equally present here? The questions hung like lead in midair, heavy and impenetrable. The porter simply kept shaking his head and shrugging his shoulders. No answer was necessary. That's just the way it was.

It isn't that we didn't get lunch; it's that where we would be allowed to eat was even a problem that bothered me. This was not an isolated incident of this attitude. On the Mount Athos monastery in Greece, I was told, they didn't even permit female animals. The very sight of a female, any female, disturbs men, it seems. And the holier the man, the greater the disturbance, apparently. It ought to be, I thought, exactly the opposite.

The question of the place of women in the church did not emerge for me with the advent of Gloria Steinem and Simone de Beauvoir. The truth is that at that time, I had yet to read either of them. No, I had confronted the issue years before they came along to tell me that I'd been right all along about my concerns. One of my cousins was the bishop's pageboy. I wasn't even allowed on the altar, unless, of course, I was cleaning the church floor on Saturday. Sister ran the school but Father had the last word about everything we did. Women put on all the church parties but men were the ushers and wore the great plumed hats and marched in the processions and carried the candles and crosses and canopy that covered the Blessed Sacrament as the priest carried it down the aisle. Men were in the church; women were in the church hall. I knew early on in life that there was a problem. A serious one. But no one said so out loud.

In regard to men and women, the church was no different from the rest of the world, and that was the problem. In the church I expected to see a model of the reign of God, a template of the way things would be in heaven, a sign of the way God wanted things to be on earth. Instead, the church told me that God was the problem. God had made women but clearly did not want to traffic with women directly — to wit, the Bible stories they read to us about Abraham and Moses and David and the apostles. No mention of the angel who came to announce that Sarah was to be blessed outside the natural order of things. Not a word about the exploits and contributions to the economy of salvation in Judith or Deborah or Esther or Naomi or Ruth. No talk of Martha's messianic proclamation, only Peter's. No notice that the rabbi taught theology to a woman at the Samaritan well. No awareness that Mary was treated as a free agent in the birth of Christ. No memory of the women at the foot of the cross, at the announcement of the empty tomb to the men who should have been there. No understanding that the church took root in house churches started and presided over by women. They gave us half a Scripture, half a history, half a worldview, and told us that it was all there was.

Indeed, it was a bare and sterile church for you if you were a girl. Even most of the sisters, the only image I had of a woman doing church, took the names of male saints. And why not, when — as I learned years later from a church historian — 75 percent of the canonized saints of the church were men? The message was clear: the church was a male preserve. Eucharist was the acme of the faith and the sacraments were required of both women and men, of course, but women could not expect to have either Eucharist or sacraments unless there was a man around who was willing to provide them. Clearly, there was a pale, even in the church, and women were outside of it.

Women scholars, many of them certified by the secular academic system around them, began to ask, "Can a male Savior save women?" It's a poignant question. After all, if Jesus as male is so utterly other than a female — not simply human, not merely divinity become present in fleshly form — are women really saved at all? Slowly, slowly I began to ask myself a different question: Could a woman really be a Catholic at all? Or are we, as we were at the meeting in Rome, simply observers? The fullness of the faith was surely not meant for us. And that, according to Roman catechesis, was because God wanted it that way, and much as they might like, they could not do otherwise. So surely God, too, does not really want us. Not really. Not completely. So why would a woman be there?

The answer came out of the stuff of the question itself: God. I no more believed that God made women half human, half capable of grace, half available to the divine than I believed that no one else except Catholics went to heaven or that those who were not white were not fully human or that we could perpetrate whatever violence we chose on anyone else whom we named lesser than ourselves and call it holy. I did not believe in a God who created half the human race in order to reject it.

I did believe in the Jesus of my daily *lectio,* who clearly walked with women and with men equally. I did believe in the world of equals that this Jesus believed in, died for. I did believe that God works through everything and that the church, which treasures the memory of creation and salvation, will someday grow into it. I believed in the church that grew finally, finally past the Crusades, and the Inquisition, and a science that was mythology. I believed in questioning the unquestionable so that the answers we gave ourselves would look more like the answers that lived in a Jesus whose questions were also not acceptable.

Until the church answers the women's question in a way that makes the gospel real and all of humanity human, the integrity of its sacraments, its theology, and its structures are all at stake. It is the question that will not go away, for it makes every other dimension of the faith either true or false. Either baptism makes new people of us all or it does not. Either we are all receptacles of grace or we are not. Either incarnation redeems all of us or it does not. Either what the church teaches about the redemption of the flesh — all flesh, female as well as male — in Jesus is true or it is false. Either Jesus became flesh or he became only male. Either we are all responsible for the deposit of faith or we are not.

When the women's movement emerged from the hibernation

caused by the gain of the vote, women with questions were standing there waiting for it. When Pope John XXIII named feminism as one of the signs of the times and a church that had forever denied women thus found itself facing the biggest women's question of them all, women were standing there waiting for the church which had taught them the answer to their own question to make real a theology which until now had been only theoretical. We were all waiting all our lives, whether we realized it consciously or not. And we are waiting still. I among them.

And More Questions to Come

A series of things has happened that raised another question in me. The first happened long ago, gestated for years, and is only now becoming plain in its implications. One of my most long-standing memories of the wrestling match between reason and feeling came to me as a young nun when reason (the objective adherence to the rules of the game) reigned, and feeling (the error of the particular) was a failure to be avoided if a person was to be truly strong, truly holy. When the telephone rang in our priory that day, none of us was prepared for the response to it.

The mother of Eileen Condon, a seventeen-year-old junior in the local parochial school, had just been found dead on her kitchen floor. There was one other girl in the family, a younger Down's syndrome child, and no father. A sad and shocking situation, surely, but no immediate concern of ours. After all, we were nuns. In our commitment to separation from the world, we didn't go into people's homes. Good nuns stayed in their convents, kept the rule, and prayed.

I saw her get up from the community room table and go to the shawl cupboard. "I don't know when I'll be back," she said. "Take phone numbers." The superior sat at the head of the table. "Where are you going, Sister Lois Marie?" she asked. "To the Condons," Lois said, adjusting her shawl. "You can't do that without permission," the superior said. "I'll call Erie and ask Mother Alice if it's all right for you to go." By this time, Lois was on her way down the hall. "Fine," she called back. "You call if you want to, but I'm going there regardless. I do not intend to leave that child alone." I heard the back door close and felt my stomach lurch. "How could she possibly do that?" I asked myself. As the years went by I knew that the real question was, How could the rest of us not? The answer to that question has become more and more clear as the years have gone by. We, as a culture, have repressed feeling to the point where law supersedes love and people without feelings make the laws. We act as if a world that operates without feeling could somehow live a higher law.

The second impetus in my quest for a resolution of the tension between reason and feeling came with the statement of Pope John Paul II that women had "a special vocation" for which they were uniquely fitted. I resented the comment at the time as simply another way of saying that the purpose of women was primarily and solely to bear children, despite the fact that even those who do, do so for only a very small portion of their lives. But I have begun to think other of the insight now. I have begun to see how dearly we need in society what we have suppressed in our idolization of a male culture and the value system it spawns. We train young people to sit at the bottom of nuclear missile silos and when the light goes to green to press the buttons that will annihilate the world without ever seeing the faces of their enemies. We abstract feeling from the rationality of war and do grossly irrational things as a result. We plot economy in terms of profit figures and have no feeling for the pain, the starvation, caused by our "cyclical corrections." We "downsize" our businesses with no care for the feelings of the long-time workers whose lives are ruined by them. We put no faces on our graphs. We allow no feelings to affect the figures we use to chart our growth curves. We abstract feeling from decision making and call ourselves "objective." We equate feelings with women and so diminish both.

Better to save money on Medicare than save a baby's life. Better to pay people less for fewer hours than hire people full time and be required to pay them benefits. Better to put money into the military than into education. These are the "sensible" things to do. These are the rational things to do. These are the things that are good for profit, good for power, good for the economy, good for a few. Better to absorb a little pain in the workers and the women and the children who will be affected by such strategies than to let feelings interfere with thought. Better to wed money and power than intuition and integrity. Better to ignore the results of our plans than violate the rules of the game. Better to make money than to make things right. Better to sell out the dream than to admit that we are making a social nightmare with our politics of selfishness played out in the name of personal freedom and economic growth. Better to be pragmatic than to listen to the cries of those who have committed their lives to ideals rather than rationality.

What is it that leads a whole system to breach its own integrity, its own purpose? What is it that leads us to choose short-term profits over long-term values? Whatever happened to the notion that "it is better to lose in a cause that must someday succeed than to succeed in a cause that must someday fail"? What is it that leads us to barter the petty for the holy?

It defrauds the human spirit, this lack of regard for the feelings of those who suffer and the feelings of those who feel for them. It is a signal of the depth and gravity of the spiritual question that is even now looming on the horizon of the human soul. The fact is that we have gone as far as rationality will take us. Rationality and the power to enforce it gave us the *encomienda* system, slavery, segregation, sexism, religious intolerance, nuclearism, and ecological ruin. It has drained the soul of feeling for the truly human, human concerns.

The papal statement is surely correct, however inadequate the present response to such an obvious truth. Women do have something to bring to the world that the world has too long eschewed. Women are expected to provide feeling in the private arena but are denied the right to bring it to the public arena, where it is so obviously missing. Blamed for being "irrational" and "too emotional," women may be the only hope we have to redeem rationality and bring the grace of feeling to the ruthlessness of pure thought. They may be all we have left that can once again show us, men and women alike, what it is to be fully human. If feeling is not affirmed in women and released in men, if reason is not tempered by feeling in men and brought to wholeness in women, we all are surely doomed spiritually. The Jesus who taught wept. The Jesus who preached played with children. The Jesus who spoke hard prophetic words spoke loving, kind ones, too. The Jesus who walked with men also talked with women.

More than that, if reason and feeling are not soon balanced in the public arenas of our world, in congresses and consistories alike, we may also be doomed physically. We must now begin to integrate reason and feeling or we confine ourselves to the paucity of the human mind and the sterility of the soul that comes with the denial of sensitivities. We have taken the objective, the emotionless, the pragmatic, the powerful to the ultimate. We have wrung the human soul dry of the kind of thinking that feeling brings.

Consequently, we now face the question of the tension between the catechetical and the mystical, the dogmatic and the spiritual, that is infecting every dimension of modern life. We want rules and dogmas and systems and hierarchies so that we can tell who has the power, who's right and who's wrong, who's on top and who doesn't count at all. That way we can dispose of the earth, the animals, and the women without contest and call all of it God's will.

Until feeling becomes as important as thinking, as important to the spiritual life as rituals and rules, we will continue to have religion but we will never find spirituality, we will have countries but we will never have culture, we will have liturgy but we will never have holiness, we will have religious life but we will never have religious.

Until we concern ourselves with how people will feel as a result of what we do, we have not really thought a thing through — at all. Feeling is not non-thinking. Feeling is another way of thinking. Feeling may be the only thing that, in the end, can finally take us beyond the structures and politics and shifting dogmas of the church into the heart of God.

Epilogue

None of the questions that have consumed my life is completely answered, of course. We are still struggling to bridge religious differences. We have yet to define social sin adequately. We are still in search of peace in an increasingly brutal world. We are still dealing with a male power structure everywhere. We have yet to deal with the role of women in the church in a theologically persuasive and coherent way. And we are only beginning to recognize that we are spiritually crippled by the fact that we fail to bring the godliness of feeling to our most serious thoughts and policies and plans and programs. But each of the questions has, at least, come to a head in my lifetime. Some of them are even showing signs of resolution: the Catholics and the Lutherans have signed an accord that says that it was all a great misunderstanding and, yes, Lutherans can go to heaven. I have prayed in international meetings and even on Catholic altars with Buddhist and Hindu friends in whose eyes I see the light of God. The Catholic bishops wrote a peace pastoral affirming the religious commitment to conscientious objection. Ten years ago I taught at a Catholic university whose male students swore that there was no such thing as sexism on their campus. Their men's losing basketball teams played to full bleachers for the entire season, however, while their girl's championship team played to empty gymnasiums night after winning night. Now, both men and women pack public arenas to watch women play professional ball. The church has accepted altar girls and women eucharistic ministers, at least, even if not ordained deaconesses yet. And women around the world are beginning to organize to gain the rights that any human being deserves.

Nevertheless, even though I realize that all of my questions are admittedly a long way from resolution, Plato said something else that convinces me that I would rather be asking them than not. "Everything that deceives," Plato said, "can be said to enchant." I have been enchanted by far too many falsehoods in life. I would rather go on living the struggle than go comatose in the face of answers that are not true, were never true, cannot possibly be true. Most of all, I have indeed found that the very process of examining them has made my life worthwhile.

In one way or another, all the people whose writing appears in this collection have been part of this process of reflection. I have seen in them parts of my own answers, fragments of my own questions. I am more grateful than they know for the guidance they have been to me along the way. I am most grateful for the work they have done here to show us all the way to the power of the questions to come to change our own small lives.

Books by Joan D. Chittister, OSB

The Friendship of Women: A Spiritual Tradition. Erie, Pa.: Benetvision, 2000.

Living Well. Maryknoll, N.Y.: Orbis Books, 2000.

The Story of Ruth. Grand Rapids: Eerdmans, 2000.

The Illuminated Life. Maryknoll, N.Y.: Orbis Books, 2000.

Gospel Days: Reflections for Every Day of the Year. Maryknoll, N.Y.: Orbis Books, 1999.

In Search of Belief. Liguori, Mo.: Liguori/Triumph, 1999.

Light in the Darkness: New Reflections on the Psalms. New York: Crossroad, 1998.

Heart of Flesh: A Feminist Spirituality for Women and Men. Grand Rapids: Eerdmans, 1998.

Songs of Joy: New Meditations on the Psalms. New York: Crossroad, 1997.

A Passion for Life: Fragments of the Face of God. Maryknoll, N.Y.: Orbis Books, 1996.

The Fire in These Ashes. Kansas City, Mo.: Sheed & Ward, 1996.

The Psalms: Meditations for Every Day of the Year. New York: Crossroad, 1996.

Beyond Beijing: The Next Step for Women. Kansas City, Mo.: Sheed & Ward, 1996.

There Is a Season. Maryknoll, N.Y.: Orbis Books, 1995.

In a High Spiritual Season. Liguori, Mo.: Triumph, 1995.

The Rule of Benedict: Insights for the Ages. New York: Crossroad, 1992.

Wisdom Distilled from the Daily: Living the Rule of St. Benedict Today. San Francisco: HarperCollins, 1990.

Womanstrength: Modern Church, Modern Women. Kansas City, Mo.: Sheed & Ward, 1990.

Job's Daughters: Women and Power. New York: Paulist Press, 1990.

Winds of Change: Women Challenge the Church. Kansas City, Mo.: Sheed & Ward, 1986.

Psalm Journal I. Kansas City, Mo.: Sheed & Ward, 1985.

Psalm Journal II. Kansas City, Mo.: Sheed & Ward, 1985.

Woman, Ministry and the Church. New York: Paulist Press, 1983.

Faith and Ferment: An Interdisciplinary Study of Christian Beliefs and Practices. Joan Chittister and Martin Marty. Minneapolis: Augsburg, 1983.

Living the Rule Today: A Series of Conferences on the Rule of Benedict. Erie, Pa.: Benet Press, 1982.

Climb along the Cutting Edge: An Analysis of Change in Religious Life. Joan Chittister et al. New York: Paulist Press, 1977.

Contributors

TISSA BALASURIYA, OMI, is the founder and director of the Center for Society and Religion in Colombo, Sri Lanka. He is also the author of *Planetary Theology, Eucharist and Human Liberation,* and *Mary and Human Liberation.*

DANIEL BERRIGAN, SJ, is a Jesuit priest and poet, well known for his witness for peace. Among his many books are *The Bride, Ezekiel,* and *Uncommon Prayer.*

BROTHER THOMAS BEZANSON is a Benedictine monk and ceramic artist with works in national and international museum collections. An American born in Nova Scotia, he holds a graduate degree in philosophy from the University of Ottawa, Canada, and is presently artist-in-residence with the Benedictine Sisters of Erie.

KENNETH A. BRIGGS is a former religion editor for the *New York Times* and former religion writer for *Newsday.* Currently he is a free-lance writer and columnist for Beliefnet, whose book on American nuns since Vatican II, *Holy Siege,* is forthcoming.

GAIL GROSSMAN FREYNE is cofounder of the Family Therapy and Counselling Centre in Dublin, Ireland. She holds a law degree from the University of Melbourne, Australia, an M.A. in women's studies from University College Dublin, and is currently engaged in doctoral research on ecological feminist philosophy and the role of care and justice in ethical reflection.

MATTHEW FOX is President of the University of Creation Spirituality in downtown Oakland, and director of the Naropa University Master's Program in Creation Spirituality. He is the author of twenty-four books including, *Original Blessing, The Reinvention of Work, Sheer Joy: Conversations with Thomas Aquinas on Creation Spirituality,* and *Illuminations of Hildegard of Bingen.*

THOMAS C. FOX, publisher of the *National Catholic Reporter,* was its editor from 1980 to 1996. He has written for numerous publications and is the author of four books, including *Sexuality and Catholicism.*

Currently he is working on a book about the local Catholic churches of Asia.

EDWINA GATELEY is an independent Catholic minister who founded the international Volunteer Missionary Movement and Genesis House in Chicago. She is also an author, an internationally recognized public speaker, and an advocate for women struggling to leave a lifestyle of prostitution.

IVONE GEBARA is a feminist philosopher and theologian who lives and works in the northeast of Brazil. She is a lecturer and workshop leader on feminist and ecological concerns in Brazil and around the world.

THOMAS J. GUMBLETON is the Auxiliary Bishop of the Archdiocese of Detroit. His passionate, nonviolent commitment to the gospel of peace and justice is the signature gift of his ministry in the Roman Catholic church.

DIANA L. HAYES is Associate Professor of Systematic Theology at Georgetown University. She was the first African American woman to earn a doctorate in sacred theology from the Catholic University of Louvain, Belgium. The author of five books, she specializes in black, womanist, and liberation theologies in the United States.

ELIZABETH A. JOHNSON, CSJ, is Distinguished Professor of Theology at Fordham University. An active teacher, writer, and lecturer, she links the richness of the Catholic heritage with questions arising from present joys and sufferings. Her books include *She Who Is* and *Friends of God and Prophets.*

ROBERT F. KEELER writes about religion for *Newsday.* In 1996 he received a Pulitzer Prize for a series of stories about St. Brigid's, a Long Island Catholic parish. In 1992 he voted for Joan Chittister for president of the United States.

MARY LOU KOWNACKI, OSB, is the Director of Communications for the Benedictine Sisters of Erie and Executive Director of the Inner-City Neighborhood Art House. She has written numerous articles on nonviolence and spirituality. Her most recent book of poetry is *Prayers for a New Millennium,* from Liguori Publications.

MARY JOHN MANANZAN is a Missionary Benedictine Sister. She obtained her Ph.D. in philosophy from the Gregorian University and is the President of St. Scholastica's College, Manila, Philippines, where she also directs the Institute of Women's Studies. She is National Chairperson of GABRIELA, a national women's network and

Executive-Secretary-Treasurer of EATWOT, the Ecumenical Association of Third World Theologians.

MARTIN E. MARTY is the Fairfax M. Cone Distinguished Service Professor Emeritus at the University of Chicago and the George B. Caldwell Senior Scholar-in-Residence at the Park Ridge Center for the Study of Health, Faith, and Ethics. He is an ordained Lutheran minister and the author of many books, including the three-volume *Modern American Religion.*

RICHARD P. MCBRIEN is Crowley-O'Brien-Walter Professor of Theology at the University of Notre Dame. He is also the author of a number of books, including *Catholicism, Lives of the Popes* and the forthcoming *Lives of the Saints,* all published by HarperCollins.

PATRICIA M. MISCHE is the cofounder and President Emerita of Global Education Associates. She is the Lloyd Professor of Peace Studies and World Law at Antioch College. Her many published works include *Toward a Human World Order* (with Gerald Mische), *Star Wars and the State of Our Souls,* and the forthcoming *Religions and World Order.*

DIARMUID O'MURCHU is a social psychologist and a member of the Sacred Heart Missionary Congregation. His main ministry is that of counselor to homeless people in London's East End. He travels and lectures internationally, and his works include *Quantum Theology, Reclaiming Spirituality, Poverty, Celibacy and Obedience,* and *Religion in Exile,* all published by Crossroad.

RICHARD ROHR is a Franciscan priest and founder of the New Jerusalem Community in Cincinnati and the Center for Action and Contemplation in New Mexico.

SANDRA M. SCHNEIDERS is Professor of New Testament and Christian Spirituality at the Jesuit School of Theology and the Graduate Theological Union in Berkeley, where she has taught since 1975. A national and international lecturer, she has published seven books and is a member of the Sisters, Servants of the Immaculate Heart of Mary of Monroe, Michigan.

JANET MARTIN SOSKICE is University Lecturer in Theology at the University of Cambridge, Fellow of Jesus College, and past President of the Catholic Theological Association of Great Britain.

CHRISTINE VLADIMIROFF, OSB, is Prioress of the Benedictine Sisters of Erie. She holds a Ph.D. in Latin American studies. From 1991 to

1998 she was the President and CEO of Second Harvest National Network of Food Banks. From 1981 to 1991 she served as the Secretary of Education for the Diocese of Cleveland.

ELAINE M. WAINWRIGHT is a Sister of Mercy of Brisbane, Australia. She lectures in biblical studies and feminist theology in the Catholic Theological College of the Brisbane College of Theology. A national and international lecturer, she has published two books and numerous articles.

REMBERT G. WEAKLAND, former Archabbot of St. Vincent in Latrobe, Pennsylvania, and Abbot Primate of the Benedictine Confederation, has been Archbishop of Milwaukee since 1977.